The Debate on the the Rise of the British Empire

ANTHONY WEBSTER

MANCHESTER
UNIVERSITY PRESS

MANCHESTER AND NEW YORK

distributed exclusively in the USA by Palgrave

The right of Anthony Webster to be identified as the author of this work has been asserted by him in accordance with the Copyright, Designs and Patents Act 1988.

Published by Manchester University Press
Oxford Road, Manchester M13 9NR, UK
and Room 400, 175 Fifth Avenue, New York, NY 10010, USA
www.manchesteruniversitypress.co.uk

Distributed exclusively in the USA by
Palgrave, 175 Fifth Avenue, New York,
NY 10010, USA

Distributed exclusively in Canada by
UBC Press, University of British Columbia, 2029 West Mall,
Vancouver, BC, Canada V6T 1Z2

British Library Cataloguing-in-Publication Data
A catalogue record for this book is available from the British Library

Library of Congress Cataloging-in-Publication Data applied for

ISBN 0 7190 6792 8 *hardback*
EAN 978 0 7190 6792 1

ISBN 0 7190 6793 6 *paperback*
EAN 978 0 7190 6793 8

First published 2006

15 14 13 12 11 10 09 08 07 06   10 9 8 7 6 5 4 3 2 1

Typeset by Action Publishing Technology Ltd, Gloucester
Printed in Great Britain by
Bell & Bain Ltd, Glasgow

Issues in Historiography

General editor
R. C. RICHARDSON
University of Winchester

The Debate on the Rise of the British Empire

Manchester University Press

CONTENTS

*This book is dedicated to those denied the opportunity
to enjoy the study of history*

GENERAL EDITOR'S FOREWORD

History without historiography is a contradiction in terms. No historian writes in isolation from earlier work on the same subject, nor can the historian stand aloof from the insistent pressures, priorities and demands of the present. Though historians address the past they always do so in ways that are shaped – consciously or unconsciously as the case may be – by the society and systems of their own day and they communicate their findings in ways that are intelligible and relevant to a reading public consisting of their own contemporaries. For these reasons the study of history is concerned not with dead facts and sterile, permanent verdicts but with dialogues, disagreements, and controversies among its presenters, and with the changing methodologies and discourse of the subject over time. *Issues in Historiography* is a series designed to address such matters by means of case studies.

Imperialism was for such a long period a major component of Britain's identity; so much of this country's history verges on the inexplicable without reference to the imperial context. The advantages and disadvantages of empire were variously perceived and rehearsed at different moments, not least because the British Empire was anything but a fixed entity. Unsurprisingly, historians – always tuned in to their changing times – have been key figures in the long-running discourse of empire. Indeed some of them – Froude, Seeley and Hobson, for example, in the nineteenth and early twentieth century – helped define the imperial ethos. In different circumstances, as the maintenance and sustainability of empire were increasingly called into question, historians again entered the debate. They have continued to have a conspicuous presence in the discourse of the post-colonial age. In fact, the demise of the British Empire in itself has stimulated generations of new historians to look afresh at the whole imperial experience. Thus imperial history today is very much alive and well as the flourishing and voluminous Manchester University Press series *Studies in Imperialism* and the recent *Oxford History of the British Empire* amply demonstrate.

Anthony Webster confidently takes on a big subject in this book and offers a judicious guide to its complex historiography. Within a broadly chronological framework he highlights the changing grounds of debate on the British Empire and the shifting centres of interest. The varied contributions of key writers on the subject – Marx, Hobson, Lenin, Said, Colley, Cannadine, and MacKenzie *et al.* – are all properly contextualised. The historiography of Imperialism, of course, has its own distinctive features, and this volume brings them out very clearly. In other respects the historiography of Imperialism forms a case study of the general development of historical thinking and writing. The growth of social history, 'history from below', and the history of gender, to name but three twentieth-century trends, are all exhibited here in an imperial setting.

R. C. Richardson
May 2005

PREFACE

The opportunity to write a general introduction to the historiography of the rise of the British empire first presented itself through contacts with Manchester University Press initiated by my colleague at Edge Hill, Kevern Verney, for whose initial suggestion and advice I here record my gratitude. For over ten years now I have taught a second year undergraduate module on the British empire, and the chance to publish a specialised volume which could both utilise the experience gained from this, and provide a useful volume for future students of empire, was simply too good to pass up. The research and writing of the volume in itself has served to sharpen my focus on the subject, and I think, has improved the quality of my teaching.

Indeed the theme of the book is close to my heart. As a student at the University of Birmingham in the 1970s I found myself immersed in British imperial history. I was extremely fortunate to be taught by those towering figures, Anthony Hopkins and Peter Cain, who introduced, then guided me through the complexities of the subject in my last two years as an undergraduate. Peter Cain and Ian Brown, now of SOAS, took me through my PhD on British imperialism in southeast Asia, with Tom Tomlinson, also now of SOAS, providing additional help and advice. I was thus lucky enough to encounter some of the keenest minds in the field, just as they were making major contributions to it. Whatever merits are to be found in this book owe much to their influence. Any errors of omission or commission are, of course, entirely my own.

Inevitably there are many debts to acknowledge. All of those mentioned above have indirectly contributed to this work, and I gratefully offer thanks. Professor Roger Richardson's advice, encouragement and guidance has been invaluable in helping me put together a coherent manuscript. I would also like to thank my good friend Stuart Bradbury, whose comments enabled me to sharpen my prose. His wit and irreverence sparked much laughter and made light the sometimes mundane task of redrafting. Edge Hill's support for my research over many years must also be acknowledged. Last, but not least I must thank my wife Lesley, whose love, encouragement, tolerance and patience have been the real inspiration of my work over many years. Without her I would have achieved little.

Anthony Webster
Edge Hill

1

The British empire: an enduring fascination

At the beginning of the twenty-first century, popular and academic interest in Britain's imperial past remains as strong as ever. Over forty years after Harold Macmillan's 'winds of change' speech, which signalled official recognition that Britain was moving into a post-imperial era of second-class power status, debate still rages among historians about the origins and significance of the empire upon which 'the sun never set'. Reasons for this enduring fascination are not difficult to identify. Uncertainty about the future of the nation-state in an era of globalisation, Britain's compromised sovereignty within the European Union and its post imperial international role of 'Robin' to America's 'Batman' have prompted reflection on Britain's former position of imperial dominance, tinged for some with feelings of nostalgia. Increasingly awkward questions about the Union of England, Wales, Scotland and Northern Ireland, following over a century of turbulence and secession in Ireland, and more recent devolutions of power to Wales, Scotland and Northern Ireland, has focused attention on the roots of that Union, and the role of imperial aspiration and empire in its origins. In this way, the British empire has moved from the periphery to the centre of the British experience, from considerations of its impact upon and legacy for the world, to its significance for the very creation of Britain itself. The peculiar separation by historians of British domestic history from the nation's imperial past, commented upon so widely by historians now, is being challenged by the momentum of recent events.[1] The heightened awareness of national identities in the UK, encouraged both by the European dilemma for national sovereignty, and the loosening of control from Westminster, has also prompted reflection on the origins of 'Britishness' and its connections with empire. The human legacy in Britain also prompts attention to the imperial age. The post-war waves of immigration from the empire and Commonwealth, and the multi-ethnic society they bequeathed, will remain lasting, immediate and physical signifiers of empire for generations born long after its demise.

There is also a sense in which the Establishment and people of Britain remain, at least in part, in denial about the demise of empire. In spite of Macmillan's implied capitulation of imperial and world power status in 1959, and the bleak realities of imperial withdrawal following the economic crises of the 1960s, sporadic but volcanic eruptions of imperial fervour still dot the historical landscape of the post-imperial era. Many who witnessed in 1982 the crowds singing *Rule Britannia* on the dockside in Southampton, to welcome troops returning from the recapture of the Falkland Islands from Argentina, could not avoid the impression that some deeply hidden conviction of national superiority and destiny had been unleashed. The most usual channel for such pretensions has been Britain's supporting role for the successor to the imperial mantle, the USA. Active, though junior, military involvement in Iraq (1991 and 2003), Kosovo (2000) and Afghanistan (2002), have all helped sustain this British self image of special importance in world affairs. As an English-speaking former colony displaying strong cultural ties with the 'old country', the US has been seen by some as the natural and appropriate inheritor of the imperial role, an idea mooted by Winston Churchill and championed by a popular historical television series on the empire.[2] Indeed, academic historians have detected parallels between the British empire and its American successor, especially in the exercise of indirect control through economic or cultural means, rather than formal conquest.

This book on the unfolding debate about the roots of British imperialism is therefore timely. Current fascination with the British empire and its origins is not a new phenomenon. From the early days of imperial expansion in the seventeenth century, through the high point of imperial power in the Victorian and Edwardian era, down to the years of decolonisation in the 1950s and 60s, and the post-imperial decades, successive generations of historians and commentators have offered their own interpretations of the reasons for Britain's rise to global dominance, and the effects of it upon those on the receiving end of British power. The re-evaluation of historical movements and events by new generations is not of course restricted to Britain's imperial past, but few subjects have stimulated such a varied response. For some nineteenth-century British historians, the empire was a force for good in the world, celebrated both for its civilising influence over the 'backward' regions, and its role in refining and elevating the British character. In contrast, the historiography of empire in the post-colonial period is largely critical or condemnatory, denouncing imperialists as brutal exploiters of subject peoples, who justified themselves by crude racist depictions of the conquered as inferior beings. The book will take us through the evolving explanations and perspectives of empire from the earliest times; from the mercantilist justifications of the seventeenth and eighteenth centuries, through the triumphalism of the late Victorian era, to the analytical and critical dissections of empire in the late and post-colonial periods. It will provide an understanding of the development of historical thought about the empire, equipping the reader with the critical tools to tackle the complexities of the shifting debate.

The opening two chapters will set the context for a detailed exploration of the academic debate about the origins of the British empire, while each following chapter outlines and engages with a key interpretation or approach to the subject. Chapter 2 will give a brief outline of the growth of the empire from the sixteenth to the early twentieth century, together with a survey of various theoretical explanations and justifications offered by commentators from the early mercantilists, to apologist historians of the late Victorian period such as Froude and Seeley.[3] This first, brief chapter, however, will consider more closely the problems surrounding the concept of imperialism, and its many definitions. It will also consider why the British among the various continental European empires, has attracted so much interest and controversy among historians.

The debate about imperialism in general has been complicated by the inability of historians to agree upon a precise meaning of the term. All concur that in the modern context it refers to the exercise of superior power by a nation-state over weaker nations or territories, but beyond that opinions diverge markedly. Most dictionary definitions take their cue from older interpretations of the word, namely the direct rule of foreign territories by a dominant state, under the authority of an emperor.[4] This definition of 'formal' empire as the imposition of direct governance of a territory or nation by the imperial power, was the commonly accepted use of the term for most observers of empire until the 1950s, though a wider interpretation of the word can be detected in some accounts.[5] It was only in the 1950s, however, that a broader definition began to be consciously employed, particularly by the Oxbridge historians John Gallagher and Ronald Robinson.[6] For them, formal empire was supplemented by 'informal empire', which involved the application of imperial coercion over subject states without the use of either overwhelming military force, or the imposition of direct rule. The economic dependence on the imperial power of superficially sovereign states, or their fear of conquest, were powerful levers which allowed imperialists to secure the installation or co-operation of compliant indigenous governments. In this way all the advantages of imperial rule, including access to markets and raw materials or the protection of vulnerable colonial borders, could be ensured without incurring the related financial and human costs of conquest. For Gallagher and Robinson, this was the mode of imperial rule which the parsimonious Victorian British state preferred, because it minimised risk as well as expense, and helped to keep taxes low.

As appealing as the concept of 'informal empire' is however, it has fuelled disagreement over the meaning of imperialism. While there are some clear examples of the exertion of informal power over supposedly sovereign states, in other cases historians have doubted either the degree of imperial incursion into the subordinate state, or the ability of the imperialists to actually exert their power when circumstances so demanded. D. C. M. Platt, an early critic of the Gallagher and Robinson thesis, questioned the degree of economic incursion into continents such as Africa and Latin America in the early nineteenth century, which Gallagher and Robinson had suggested was sufficient to create a relationship of dependency of the African and South American polities (periphery) on Britain (the metropole).[7] Platt argued that the British lacked both the economic leverage and the will to turn these entities into true components of their empire. Sceptics have argued that the informality of some alleged imperialist relationships stretch to the point where it is hard to discern a clear imbalance of power between the nations concerned. After all, power relations between nations fluctuate over time and from issue to issue; national supremacy in some areas is frequently counterbalanced by a deficit in others. As a result, there are many instances where it is difficult to clearly identify international relationships as imperialistic in nature. Since the Second World War, for example, many on the left have claimed that Britain is part of an informal American empire, an accusation given fresh import during recent international crises. Yet the requirement that many aspects of British law and economic policy formation conform to the rules of membership of the European Union might just as easily lead to the conclusion that it is the emergent supranational European super state which now exerts the decisive imperial power over London. At times, informal empire can seem a nebulous and questionable label.

Disagreements over definitions of imperialism inevitably become entangled with differences over root causes. Lenin, for example, saw the 'New Imperialism' of the late nineteenth century as a function of capitalist economic development, to the extent that he defined imperialism as a stage in that process of economic change. For those who remained unconvinced by both Marxism and economic explanations of imperialism, this could never be acceptable. The definition of those on the right like Arthur Balfour, who saw Britain's imperial supremacy as the inevitable and natural expression of western racial and cultural superiority, was equally unpalatable for those on the left.[8] Some recent analysts of imperialism have come to define the concept as a cultural or psychological one, a mental predisposition towards conquest nurtured by an aggressively supremacist western culture. Edward Said's damning critique of western culture's jaundiced stereotype of the despotic and primitive cultures of the Orient, started a new trend of imperial writing which focuses upon the mindset of empire, the beliefs, attitudes and cultural assumptions which incline European and western countries towards imperial conquest.[9] These cultural explanations and definitions of imperialism have themselves generated robust opposition, from those who locate the origins of empire in economic rather than cultural phenomena, and from those who accuse Said and his supporters of committing the same error of which they accuse western orientalists – stereotyping and condemning whole national cultures.

But a good deal of the passion in the debate about the meaning of imperialism arises from judgements about the moral and material consequences of empire rather than intellectual differences. The peculiar moral journey of imperialism, from the Victorian celebration of empire as a great civilising mission, to the modern post-colonial era, when it is castigated for its contemporary injustices and legacy of underdevelopment and poverty, has inevitably added the spice of ethical controversy to the debate. Even in recent times, when condemnation of imperialism is the orthodoxy, there remain fierce and eminent defenders not only of the record of the British empire, but also of imperialism itself. In the wake of 11 September 2001, some historians even called for the imposition of a new western imperialism in Afghanistan and other unstable areas of the middle east, arguing that this is the only viable route to modern development and democracy for these chaotic and despotic regimes.[10] At the other extreme Robert Mugabe, the controversial President of Zimbabwe, still feels able to blame his nation's ills on the legacy of British colonial rule, decades after his country's independence. The fact that imperialism is simultaneously about power relations between nations, nationalism, race, cultural encounters and confrontations, trade, economics, military prowess and ideology, has made it an arena contested by historians, politicians, journalists and social scientists with diverse academic and moral priorities. Little wonder that the debates about the nature and consequences of imperialism remain lively and at times, vitriolic.

Within the broad academic field of imperialism, the British empire has probably attracted the greatest interest among historians. The French, German, Austro-Hungarian and Russian empires all have their own exhaustive literatures of course, but the British example stands above them. Consequently much of the theoretical debate about imperialism has centred upon the British empire, which has tended to be seen as a model for other modern imperial systems. From here, there has been a tendency to extrapolate trends observed in the British experience to other European empires, with historians seeking parallel or similar developments. Thus key concepts in imperialism such as informal empire and Said's cultural imperialism which drew principally from analysis of the British empire, have been applied to other European imperial histories. Similarly, much of the historical debate about economic theories of empire, from Hobson, Lenin, through Fieldhouse to the recent work of Cain and Hopkins, tends to identify the British variant as the principal testing ground for analysis.[11] Why has the British empire occupied such a central position in the debate about imperialism?

There are a number of reasons for this phenomenon. Firstly, the longevity of British imperialism and its evolutionary nature have been a perennial source of interest. At the time of the earliest settlement of the colonies in North America and the West Indies, Britain was a relatively sparsely populated agrarian society, still in the throes of redefining its political system through civil war and reform. By the time colonial rule was being established over Africa in the late nineteenth century, Britain was a rapidly urbanising industrial society, with a unified political system moving towards modern liberal democracy, occupying a unique position of world economic leadership. Such was the transformation of both the metropolitan society and the empire in the intervening period that many historians effectively deny imperial continuity, choosing instead to distinguish between a 'First Empire' based on an ideology of commercial monopoly and protectionism (mercantilism), and a 'Second Empire' governed mainly in accordance with the principles of free trade.[12] The loss of the American colonies in the 1770s is seen as the watershed between the two imperial experiments and much of the historical writing about empire has tended to treat the two periods as discrete areas of study. As David Armitage has recently commented, this has contributed to much misunderstanding of the empire and its relations with domestic British development.[13] In this way the sheer length of the British empire's life has added to the complexity of the debate.

A second reason for the enduring fascination with the British empire is Britain's unique position as the first modern capitalist

economy, generally seen until recently as a predominantly industrial phenomenon, but now taken to encompass the nation's
emerging role as the principal financial and commercial centre of
the world.[14] Inevitably, a good deal of the debate about the
empire has been preoccupied with the relationship between
British economic hegemony and the growth of empire, and the
question of whether empire was a help or a hindrance to the
British economy. Thus Hobson not only saw New Imperialism as
a direct consequence of the character of British economic development, he was also gravely concerned with the deleterious
consequences of empire for the future health of the metropolitan
economy. In this way, those seeking to explain the trajectory of
Britain's economic fortunes, and the reasons for alleged decline,
have also been drawn to the study of empire. Even eminent political journalists like Will Hutton have turned to the vibrant
literature on British imperialism to inform both diagnosis and
treatment of the 'British Disease'.[15] This interest in the connection between empire and economy has ensured a high profile for
British imperialism long after the end of empire.

Social developments within Britain since the middle of the
twentieth century have assisted this process. The growth of
substantial immigrant communities from former colonies in Asia
and the West Indies since the war, has brought rich but often
volatile encounters between British culture and that of their
former colonial subjects. The need to respond to racism has
helped sustain both academic and popular fascination with the
British empire, and the racial/cultural relations which it fostered,
as a means to improving inter-ethnic relations in modern Britain.
Other contemporary questions about the nature of Britain itself,
and its post-imperial role in the world, have also kept thoughts of
empire to the fore. The eruption of the chronic troubles in
Northern Ireland, almost at the very moment that the 'imperial
game' was abandoned at the end of the 1960s, helped ensure that
the imperial legacy would impact directly upon British politics,
long after the flag had been lowered in the colonies. The
campaigns for Scottish and Welsh devolution over the next
twenty years, and the progressive integration into Europe which
followed, also kept alive questions about national sovereignty and
the post-colonial viability of a United Kingdom, together with the

issue of Britain's former position as a global, imperial power. Contemplation of former glory was made the more poignant by the new global imperium of the USA. Sharing a common language, a similar political system and a heritage of military alliance in the great wars of the twentieth century made it easy for those Britons nostalgic for the days of empire to perceive continuity of its spirit in the new *Pax Americana*. The Cold War even allowed the British to maintain a shadow of former prestige, through their role as the principal ally of the Americans. Even since the fall of the Soviet Union, the British have continued to ride the coat-tails of their trans-Atlantic senior partner, leading the supporting cast for American imperial adventures in Iraq and Afghanistan. Though the financial and human costs are occasionally high, British politicians of all persuasions still cling to the trappings of global influence provided by the 'special relationship'. Occasionally this undercurrent of imperial nostalgia, this reluctance to let go of the past, bursts to the surface. The seizure of the Falkland Islands by Argentina in 1982, following British diplomatic errors and a scramble to reduce defence spending, was the last occasion for such an eruption. The war and jingoistic fervour it unleashed, and the determination to strike back regardless of pressure for a more restrained approach from the USA, were seen by some as symptomatic of a collective denial of new realities.

Finally the sheer size and diversity of the British empire at its zenith has undoubtedly contributed to the fascination. The student of the British empire confronts a rich canvas of social, economic and cultural variety. One consequence has been the proliferation of geographically specialised studies, a wealth of books and articles which focus exclusively on particular colonies. The regional diversity of the British empire has certainly justified this trend, and has produced probably the richest literature on imperialism in print. It was not merely that the empire contained such an array of different cultures, societies and political systems; it was also that British responses to them were extremely varied. It must be remembered that the British empire was assembled over several centuries, and that there were therefore temporal as well as geographical factors which contributed to the diversity of forms of rule. Structures of imperial governance which reflected aspects of the metropolitan political system and society in one era, occasionally survived as atavistic remnants regardless of change in Britain itself. Thus, for example, the East India Company staggered on as the agency of government for India well into the nineteenth century, regardless of the fact that the organisation had long ceased to be a truly commercial entity. The Company's rule was only ended because the Indian rebellion of 1857 exposed its inadequacies in government.

In fact one of the British empire's defining features was its particularism – its adaptation and adjustment of colonial institutions to meet specific local circumstances. At one extreme, the British were content to devolve a large degree of power to the local inhabitants, even conceding effective self rule within the empire. The White Dominions, particularly Canada, Australia and New Zealand were the beneficiaries of such liberal concession, which was granted on the assumption that the predominantly white and British inhabitants of these colonies needed and deserved the right of self government. It is interesting that this concession was not extended to the Irish until after much bitter conflict. Racial stereotyping ensured that brown Indians and black Africans would not enjoy such indulgence, and in these colonies direct rule through senior British officials was the norm until independence. But even here there was flexibility. The Indian princely states were treated with a 'light touch', with the appointment of British Residents to gently guide local rulers in the right direction.[16] When the Indian independence movement gathered momentum during the First World War, the British did concede limited self rule in the reforms of 1919. Frequently the assertion of direct British rule was determined and shaped by local contingencies and circumstances. After the conquest of Burma in 1885, the collapse into near chaos of local political and social institutions, forced the British to assert a most intrusive system of government, with District Officers dictating many aspects of village life. In the Malay states, the collapse of order in the 1870s following civil wars and violent feuds between rival secret societies within the Chinese tin-mining community, forced the British to install Residents to 'advise' the local Sultans; an innovation which over the next thirty years turned into creeping direct rule.[17] Then of course there were those nations and territories subjected to such a degree of political or economic pressure from the British, that many historians regard them as informal appendages of the empire. Among these was China, which by the end of the nineteenth century was so dependent upon loans from British financial institutions, and on London's determination to curb the imperial ambitions of Japan, Russia and Germany for Chinese territory, that many British officials attributed to it a quasi-colonial status. Of course, informal rule took at least as wide a variety of forms as did formal rule in the parts of the globe shaded red.

In London, this bewildering variety of governing strategies produced awkward and eccentric administrative arrangements, with an uneasy division of imperial responsibilities, especially between the India and Colonial Offices, whose senior civil servants and political heads viewed each other as rivals for resources and influence. Such tensions did not prevent the emergence of a common ethos in the management of the empire. Colonial civil servants developed a clear ideology of purpose, fashioned in the public schools of England from notions of racial superiority, patriotic fervour and a strong impulse of Christian service.[18] By the later nineteenth century, British officials were convinced (often mistakenly) of their expertise in the affairs of colonial societies, their cultures, political and religious practices, and customs. David Cannadine has charted the British practice in the later nineteenth century of, where possible, according indigenous rulers and local tradition due respect and observance.[19] Such behaviour bolstered British confidence in the subtlety of their imperial expertise, and it fostered the celebrated British self-image of fairness.

It is unsurprising, therefore, given the kaleidoscopic quality of the British empire, its ethnic and cultural diversity and the baffling varieties of its formal and informal rule, that historians of imperialism have come to regard it as the richest source of insights into the subject. It has become a testing ground for theoretical models of imperialism, a function it seems likely to continue to serve. Before addressing those aspects of this theoretical debate which concern the British empire specifically, it will first be helpful to trace both the growth of that empire from the seventeenth century, and the moral and intellectual justifications

11

and explanations offered by its makers and their contemporaries.

Notes

1 See, for example, D. Armitage, *The Ideological Origins of the British Empire* (Cambridge, 2000), pp. 14–15.
2 See Niall Fergusson, *Empire: How Britain Made the Modern World* (London, 2003).
3 J. A. Froude, 'England and her colonies' (1872), in P. J. Cain (ed.), *Empire and Imperialism: The Debate of the 1870s* (South Bend, Indiana, 1999), pp. 27–49; J. R. Seeley, *The Expansion of England* (London, 1883).
4 See, for example, the definition used by the *Concise Oxford English Dictionary* (6th edition, Oxford, 1978).
5 V. I. Lenin, *Imperialism: The Highest Stage of Capitalism* (1916) (Moscow, 1970 edition).
6 J. Gallagher and R. Robinson, 'The imperialism of free trade', *Economic History Review* 6 (1953), 1–15.
7 D. C. M. Platt, 'The imperialism of free trade: some reservations', *Economic History Review* 21 (1968), 298–306.
8 Speech of Arthur Balfour to the House of Commons, 13 June 1913.
9 E. Said, *Orientalism* (London, 1978).
10 Niall Ferguson, 'Welcome the new imperialism', *Guardian* (31 October 2001).
11 D. K. Fieldhouse, *Economics and Empire 1830–1914* (Ithaca, New York, 1973); P. J. Cain and A. G. Hopkins, *British Imperialism 1688–2000* (London, 2001).
12 See, for example, V. T. Harlow, *The Founding of the Second British Empire* (London, 1952 and 1964), 2 vols.
13 Armitage, *The Ideological Roots of the British Empire*, pp. 2–3.
14 A view of course most explicitly outlined in Cain and Hopkins, *British Imperialism*.
15 Will Hutton, *The State We're In* (London, 1996), pp. 21–2.
16 See M. H. Fisher, *Indirect Rule in India: Residents and the Residency System 1764–1858* (Oxford, 1991).
17 See A. Webster, *Gentlemen Capitalists: British Imperialism in South East Asia 1770–1890* (London, 1998), chapter 7.
18 See A. Kirk-Greene, *Britain's Imperial Administrators 1858–1966* (Basingstoke, 2000).
19 D. Cannadine, *Ornamentalism: How the British Saw Their Empire* (London, 2001).

2

Justifying British imperialism: the changing rationale of the empire builders

The reasons and motives behind the rise of the British empire have been a source of huge controversy among historians during the twentieth century. However it would be a mistake to imagine that disagreements about the purpose of empire are in any way new. Even as the empire was being built, contemporary academic and political commentators fiercely disputed the role and value of empire. From the earliest phase of imperial construction at the time of the Reformation, leading intellectuals offered a variety of different explanations, justifications and sometimes criticisms of Britain's expansionist project. This chapter will trace these early debates and theories, against the backdrop of Britain's growing empire.

While the development and growth of the British empire occurred over many centuries, it is difficult to be precise about dates without first defining what is to be included under the category of imperial expansion. In recent years there has been a tendency to redefine empire to include regions and nations within Britain itself, rather than regard it as a purely overseas phenomenon. The absorption into an English dominated 'British empire' of Wales, Scotland and Ireland inevitably carries the chronological scope of imperial conquest back into the middle ages (as early as the twelfth or thirteenth centuries), and merges debates about empire and the forging of a distinctive British national identity. Certainly historians such as David Armitage (b. 1965), Associate Professor in History at Columbia University in the USA, contend that the emergence of an imperial mentality in Britain was a process with quite distant origins in the medieval period, which built upon emerging ideas about the English monarchy's claim to suzerainty over the Scots, Irish and Welsh. According to this view, it evolved in response to a variety of developments, including the establishment of Protestantism as the dominant religion in Britain and its ongoing conflict with Catholicism, competition with rival European powers, the development of overseas commerce, and the acquisition and colonisation of territories in the new world.[1]

While this book will certainly trace some of the ideological notions of empire back to their medieval roots, it will focus principally upon the rise of Britain's overseas empire, rather than internal conquests and colonisations, which run the risk of confusing questions of national unification and external expansion. That said, the ideological roots of British imperialism will be taken back slightly further. This chapter will set the scene for the more recent debates about the reasons for the rise of the British empire which will be dealt with later in the book. It will outline the rise of the British empire from the sixteenth to the end of the nineteenth century, but the principal aim will be to explore the evolving debates among contemporaries about its value and the reasons for its expansion. It will be seen that these justifications did alter significantly over time. From the Reformation of the sixteenth century to the consolidation of Protestant dominance under William and Mary and the Hanoverian dynasty in the eighteenth century, fear that the great Catholic powers of mainland Europe would use the resource and ideological advantages wrought by overseas imperial expansion to outstrip and eventually overwhelm the Protestant kingdoms, reappeared as an underlying motive in various arguments for empire. Economic motives, closely linked to the need to preserve the integrity of the state and its official religion, were therefore prominent in thinking about empire from the outset. By the nineteenth century, economic imperatives still dominated, but the fear of Catholicism had been replaced by a desire to preserve domestic stability in the face of the turbulent social upheaval caused by industrialisation. International great power rivalry remained a constant motive, though by the end of the nineteenth century, contemporary arguments for empire were couched in terms of the modern nation state and the preservation of British hegemony in an age of rival emergent industrialising powers, rather than the starkly religious justifications of a few centuries earlier. Moral arguments for empire were increasingly founded on notions of spreading the British version of the economic and social benefits of 'western civilisation' to less developed parts of the world, rather than an exclusively Protestant, religious justification. In spite of continuities in motives and justifications for empire, it will be seen that policies for governing it did change significantly, for example the shift away from protectionism to free trade. This chapter will explore the evolution of Britain's pro-imperial ideology to the end of the nineteenth century, against a background of imperial expansion. The first half of the chapter will outline the principal developments in the rise of the empire, as a context for the exploration of imperial ideology in the second half.

Armitage identifies the first conceptualisation of a British empire in the thirteenth century, under Edward I.[2] These early notions of the unification of England, Wales, Ireland and Scotland are seen as the first articulation of the imperial idea following the Norman Conquest. These aspirations, though imperfectly and only sporadically fulfilled in the centuries which followed, were given added impetus by Henry VIII's Reformation and the establishment of a distinctive Protestant identity for the English state in the sixteenth century. This, in turn, formed the basis for the eventual 'colonisation' of Ireland by the Scots and English Protestants in the seventeenth century.[3] In this respect, Armitage argues that the processes which formed both the British state and cultural identity, were interwoven with the emergence of an imperial ideology. By the seventeenth century, when European colonisation of the American continent was beginning, the British were already in the process of developing an 'imperial mindset', in which the expansion of the kingdom and its Protestant religion were seen as a necessary step to keep pace with the parallel growth of Britain's Catholic enemies.

The growth of the overseas empire began tentatively, through officially approved commercial enterprise. Despite failed attempts at colonial settlement on the eastern seaboard of North America in the late sixteenth century, by the third decade of the seventeenth century there were small but promising outposts in Virginia, Massachusetts and Newfoundland. Two of these were backed by commercial organisations, the Virginia Company and the Massachusetts Bay Company, each of which enjoyed a measure of political support at home. Tobacco and cod were two notably successful commercial experiments in the New World, and the emerging colonial settlements were valued for the economic benefits they brought. The early pioneers of north American colonisation gained a reputation for rugged independence. This partly reflected the religious and social character of many of the early puritan settlers, whose desire to escape the stifling ideological and material constraints of Britain, set them apart from their erstwhile countrymen. As Linda Colley has also noted, limitations of wealth and power restricted the ability of the early British imperial state to interfere in the governance of the new American colonies, defining its role as 'slender and enabling rather than interventionist'.[4] By the end of the seventeenth century, the population of the American colonies had risen to approximately 260,000, a growth facilitated by the expansion of territories under British control, including the acquisition of New York from the Dutch, the founding of Pennsylvania, and extensive British settlement throughout New England, Maryland and into the Carolinas.[5] During the seventeenth century British power had also been growing in the Caribbean. By 1655 Barbados, the Leeward Islands and Jamaica had all been incorporated into the British territorial empire, and again economic considerations had been a major factor in acquisition. Caribbean sugar could bring a high price in Europe, and the development of production brought an early presentiment of the future impact of the British empire on the world – the growth of slavery and the slave trade. By 1700, of the 145,300 population of the British West Indies, over three quarters were black slaves.[6] Inevitably slavery and the slave trade expanded into the north American colonies, with the development there of tobacco and cotton production. Elsewhere, under the auspices of the East India Company, the British established a trading presence in Mughal India, first at Madras, then Bombay and Calcutta, though these were strictly commercial establishments without intention to acquire territory. Thus, by the end of the seventeenth century, the contours of a primarily Atlantic territorial empire were already well defined.

However, during the next century British imperialism underwent its first phase of major expansion. Developments in Europe
brought to the boil the simmering conflicts between the European
powers in the non-European world. Dynastic and religious
conflicts in mainland Europe were compounded by the overthrow
of the Catholic Stuart monarchy in England in 1688, and by the
accession of the new Protestant German Hanoverian dynasty after
the death of Queen Anne. The new regime were drawn into bitter
conflicts for survival with the rival European Catholic powers of
France and Spain, as well as Holland, the other main European
imperial power. These wars were truly global, encompassing
American, Asian, maritime as well as European theatres of
combat. No fewer than six major conflicts between 1689 and
1815 served to propel the British to global hegemony and the
possession of a vast overseas empire. The first of these was the
Nine Years War of 1689 to 1697, quickly followed by the War of
the Spanish Succession of 1702 to 1714. Between 1739 and 1748
the War of the Austrian Succession maintained this ongoing
confrontation with the French, but it was during the Seven Years
War of 1756 to 1763, that the British were to make crucial imperial gains. It was this conflict which delivered to them the whole
of the Eastern seaboard of North America (including eastern
Canada), as well as Bengal in India, the first foray by the East
India Company into imperial conquest. By the end of the war in
1763, the list of acquisitions was impressive. The British asserted
their dominance in North America, and added the Windward
Islands in the Caribbean to their possessions. More portentous
was that the way seemed clear for yet further territorial expansion; the great American interior seemed to beckon, and in Bengal
the British had acquired a bridgehead from which the further
extension of British rule proved irresistible. As one historian has
described it, a new phase of global empire building was at hand.[7]

Yet in the three decades which followed, setbacks seemed to
outweigh advances in the progress of the British empire. The
Seven Years War had exacted a burdensome price upon British
resources. Expanded possessions in North America had brought
additional costs of defence, made all the more essential by the
rapid growth of the thirteen north American colonies. By 1750
the white population of the American colonies had reached over

1.2 million, and continued to grow inexorably in the following decades.[8] Although British plans to maintain a standing army in America of 10,000 men were never fully realised, the costs involved in enhancing the British military presence were instrumental in forcing up the unpopular taxes on the colonists which ultimately triggered the American Revolution, and the successful overthrow of British rule by the end of the 1770s. Nor was imperial overstretch solely an American phenomenon. A critical factor in the British loss of the American colonies was the speed with which those rival European imperial powers, who had suffered at British hands earlier in the century, rallied to the cause of the American revolutionaries, confronting the British with global warfare which sapped and dissipated their resources. Even in India, where British rule in Bengal was consolidated, successfully defended and bolstered by the extension of informal influence in Awadh and Hyderabad by the end of the eighteenth century, there were ominous signs that the British had over-reached themselves. The spiralling expense of the East India Company's new role of conqueror and governor swallowed up the vast revenues of Bengal and the tribute extorted from Indian regional princes, and left it with escalating debts at home and abroad. In the 1770s and 1780s, the Company was forced to plead for financial help from the British state. It was forthcoming, but only in exchange for the imposition of strict controls over the East India Company by the British government. So began the metamorphosis of this private commercial organisation into an organ of the British imperial state. Thus by the 1790s, although the British had achieved the status of a truly global imperial power, the mood in the British body politic was deeply pessimistic.

Yet the Napoleonic wars of 1793 to 1815 transformed British apprehension and insecurity in imperial affairs into overweening confidence. The long years of global, intermittent conflict were unquestionably difficult for the British, but they brought spectacular forward movement to the frontiers of empire. With Britain's arch enemy France completely defeated, and other former rival powers such as Spain, Portugal and Holland severely weakened by the ravages of war, the British found themselves in an unprecedented position of imperial dominance. In the Caribbean, Trinidad, Tobago and St Lucia were acquired under the peace treaties of 1814–15, while in the east British rule was extended over much of southern India. Within ten years, Singapore had been established as the primary British port in south east Asia, and under the Treaty of London of 1824, the Dutch were forced to cede much of the region as the sphere of influence of the British. The acquisitions of Malta, the Ionian Isles and the Cape of Good Hope ensured the British a dominant maritime trading and military position in the Mediterranean and on the sea routes to the far east, a situation bolstered by the emphatic superiority of the Royal Navy. Economic change in Britain itself, most notably the rise of industrial production and the beginnings of the British conquest of the markets of the world, underlined and strengthened victories on the battlefield. Thus in the military, territorial and economic fields, the British emerged from war in 1815 as the leading global power, and seemed poised for yet further additions to its empire.

Yet while the two decades after the war did see considerable expansion of British formal and informal rule, it was plain that ideas and notions of empire had changed radically in Britain, in ways that promised to restrain imperial ambition. The nature of this shift can only be grasped within the wider context of the British ideological debate about empire which had been unfolding since the late middle ages. During the seventeenth and eighteenth centuries, numerous thinkers had contributed to an emerging body of ideas on empire; on what it was for and how it could be justified. By the eighteenth century these ideas came to form a quite comprehensive ideology of empire usually referred to by historians as 'mercantilism'. It was this set of ideas which came under attack during the Napoleonic wars, but before the nature of that challenge can be appreciated, the roots and rationale of mercantilism must be explored.

Perhaps the most important early contributor to mercantilist thought was Richard Hakluyt (c. 1553–1613), a scholar of the late sixteenth century. His ideas appeared in numerous publications, perhaps the most famous being his *Discourse on Western Planting* (1584) and *The Principal Navigations, Voyages, Traffiques and Discoveries of the English Nation* (1598–1600).[9] Hakluyt was in many ways the personification of the forces which drove early English colonialism. A geographer at Oxford, his interest in discoveries in the 'New World' was stimulated further by his connections with the Clothworkers Company, which between 1578 and 1586 paid him an annual pension. The company coveted Hakluyt's services because it was seeking new overseas markets, and in this respect Hakluyt represented very directly the commercial interest in overseas expansion. But Hakluyt also enjoyed political connections at the highest level which sought colonial acquisitions for purposes of state. The *Discourse on Western Planting* was no mere academic survey of the benefits of American colonisation. It was written for none other than Sir Francis Walsingham, Queen Elizabeth's trusted counsellor, whom Hakluyt advised. As such it was intended to inform government policy at a time when the threat from the Catholic powers of continental Europe was at its height, and national security dictated that Catholic imperialism should not go unchallenged in the New World.

Hakluyt argued that the great classical scholars, particularly Aristotle, had demonstrated that successful societies were those which were materially self sufficient. This was not merely a source of strength, but also of moral virtue, since only the truly self-sufficient kingdom could be free of external pressures to abandon its beliefs. It followed that if Elizabeth's Protestant kingdom was to survive in the face of Europe's hostile Catholic monarchies, it had to be economically strong and self-reliant. In an age when land was the major producer of wealth, and the prospects for raising its productivity seemed extremely limited, the only way to secure for the kingdom increased supplies of food and other commodities was by external colonisation, by acquiring new lands abroad for the kingdom. The discovery of the 'New World' offered just such an opportunity, and Hakluyt saw other potential economic advantages from the acquisition of colonies. They could act as a vent for surplus population, thereby ensuring that domestic resources would remain sufficient for the needs of the kingdom, while the migrant peoples would in turn form a market for exports, further diminishing dependence on potentially hostile foreigners.

In this way Hakluyt set out some of the main guiding principles of mercantilist thought: the need for economic self-sufficiency in a world of finite resources and competing, ideologically hostile kingdoms (in the process of evolving into nation-states), together with the notion that territorial acquisitions and their resolute defence was essential for the well-being and survival of the kingdom. Later intellectual contributions were to flesh out this framework. Samuel Purchas (*c.* 1577–1626), a biographer and scholar of Hakluyt's work, stressed the religious imperatives of empire, strengthening the notion of colonial expansion as an essential mission of Protestantism in its battle against the Papal antichrist.[10] The religious element in this emergent mercantilist philosophy was important not only in respect of justifying English Protestant imperialism as a moral counterweight to its Catholic rivals, but also in lending moral authority to the dispossession of indigenous peoples. Imperial conquest, it was argued, took the cross to heathen barbarians, in itself sufficient justification for their subordination to the will of Christians. This religious argument was supplemented later by John Locke's assertion that those better equipped to make it productive enjoyed a greater moral right to land.[11]

Numerous other writers added to this emergent mercantilist creed. During the seventeenth century the rise of the East India Company, and its attempted monopoly of trade with the east, lent credibility to mercantilist thinking. Not surprisingly, some of the most eloquent defenders of the creed were those directly involved in that organisation. Thomas Mun (1571–1641) pursued a lifelong career as a merchant in Italy and the Near East before becoming a director of the EIC in 1615. His two principal works, *Discourse of Trade from England unto the East Indies* (1621), and *Discourse on England's Treasure by Foreign* Trade (1630; published 1664) set out a defence of the East India Company's export of bullion to the east to finance the purchase of Indian commodities for the British and European markets. Sir Josiah Child (1630–99) advocated imitation of the Dutch mercantilist system of trade in his *Brief Observations Concerning Trade and the Interest of Money* (1668) and *A New Discourse of* Trade (1690). He also set out a case for Britain's assertion of monopolies of trade with her colonies. Child was also an eminent merchant and director of the EIC, as well as a prominent MP. Learned testimonies from such wealthy and high ranking figures lent mercantilist thought great authority and the backing of the state. Consequently, by the eighteenth century a clear set of principles had emerged which guided British imperial policy and relations with rival European imperial powers. At the heart of this lay the conviction that differences of religion and national character made conflict between the emerging European nations inevitable, and that policy towards the non-European world, and in economic affairs, had to reflect that fact. Conceptions of national wealth in the pre-industrial world were founded on the convictions that the world's resources and capacity for production were finite, and that the accumulation of 'treasure', meaning money or bullion, was particularly desirable, as this was a form of wealth which could easily be translated into military power.[12] The logic of this led to the development of the so-called 'balance of trade' argument in favour of colonies, which dictated that they were useful for acquiring essential raw materials and foodstuffs, thereby avoiding a drain of treasure to foreign powers to pay for such commodities.[13] The rationale which emerged from these beliefs was that nations and their sovereigns needed to acquire exclusive access to as much of the wealth producing capacity of the world as possible, and ensure that access to them was restricted as far as possible to their own nationals. Thus since monopolies on trade, and where necessary the acquisition of colonies, became integral pillars of mercantilist ideology. There was a pronounced emphasis on excluding rival nationals from participation in trade with both the colonies and those areas of the world with which the nation enjoyed supposedly exclusive trading rights. This became a firm principle of all early modern European empires. The need for a nation to protect its trade from attack, its exclusive trading privileges from infringement, and its colonies from the efforts of rivals to trade with them, implied the maintenance of a strong navy, backed by the state, which could extend as well as defend the boundaries of empire. A peculiar corollary of this was an exaggerated emphasis upon sources of wealth which were external to the home country. Increases in national wealth and power were to be achieved not so much by economic improvement and reform at home, as by new acquisitions of land and exclusive trading rights overseas. Inevitably, such ideas tilted state policies in favour of those interests connected with foreign commerce and empire, seeking to insulate them from domestic as well as foreign competition.

In the case of England, and later Britain following the Act of Union of 1707, these mercantilist notions were an established reality by the beginning of the eighteenth century. At the core were the Navigation Acts, a series of laws passed in the late seventeenth century designed to secure both Britain's grip on trade with its colonies and important markets of the world, and its ability to defend those interests by military force. The Commonwealth Navigation Act of 1651 was incorporated into the First Navigation Act of the restored monarchy in 1661. It forbade the importation of various commodities from Africa, America and Asia on ships owned by anyone other than British, natives of the country in which the commodity was produced, or natives of countries which had received the goods as first shipment. It identified sugar, cotton, tobacco and indigo as commodities to which the law would particularly apply. The Act was extended and amended by numerous revising acts in 1662, 1663, 1670, 1673 and 1696. The aim was not only to ensure that Britain would have a powerful mercantile marine, able to shepherd precious commodities into British ports, but also to develop it as an important auxiliary to the Royal Navy, providing plentiful shipping and a healthy and flourishing domestic shipbuilding industry, together with a vast body of able seamen, able to serve in the Royal Navy if required. In this way, the Navigation Acts embodied both the monopolistic and militaristic elements of mercantilist philosophy.

Another expression of mercantilist policy was the various Royal Charters granted to private companies engaged in overseas trade, bestowing upon them monopolistic rights of trade with specified parts of the world. The most important of these was the East India Company, which in 1600 was granted an exclusive trading monopoly with India and all parts of the east.[14] This monopoly was jealously guarded by the company for over two hundred years. During the course of the eighteenth century the company shifted radically away from its original remit as an organisation dedicated exclusively to trade and profit. It embarked upon wars of conquest, first in Bengal in 1757, but ultimately engulfing the whole sub-continent by the 1830s. While this metamorphosis from privileged commercial company to a militarised, state-subsidised and controlled organ of the British government was unplanned and unintended, the reasoning and priorities which drove the transformation on were essentially mercantilist in nature. Fear of rival empires (French and Dutch in this case), and the need to protect the interests of the company by force were considerations shaped by the prevailing mercantilist philosophy of the time. The eighteenth century saw the apotheosis of this mercantilist outlook, as the global European wars of the period seemed to confirm its bleak assessment of the inevitability of conflict. In a wider sense these factors embedded an enduring belief in the need for the protectionist regulation of many branches of commerce, but most particularly of essential foodstuffs. A nation which could not feed its own population would be extremely vulnerable in war, since its foreign supplies of food were vulnerable to attack. Domestic agriculture had to be protected from ruinous foreign competition to maintain its ability to meet national requirements.

Political developments in Britain itself helped to strengthen the hold of mercantilist ideas. Following the 'Glorious Revolution' of 1688, which eventually led to the downfall of the Catholic Stuart dynasty, and the sense of siege which permeated the courts of successive Hanoverian monarchs during the eighteenth century not only bolstered mercantilist perceptions of the world in governing circles, it also intensified royal dependence on those interests who benefited most from the ideology. Cain and Hopkins show how the emergence of such institutions and arrangements as the Bank of England and the National Debt proved to be crucial in enabling the Hanoverian regime to pay for effective defence without further undermining its shaky popularity at home by punitive levels of taxation.[15] This close relationship with the financiers of the City of London inevitably lent the mercantilist corporations who dominated the City considerable leverage over the determination of imperial and trading policies, and ensured that the mercantilist line would prevail.

In this way, by the middle of the eighteenth century a clear sense of a British empire, encompassing dominance of the high seas and the possession of overseas territories. was becoming an established facet of cultural life. *Robinson Crusoe* by Daniel

Defoe (1660–1731) provided an easily identifiable, popular embodiment of those perceived national characteristics which had helped found the empire. Crusoe's seafaring background, his resourcefulness in face of capture and adversity, and his easy and enlightened mastery of Friday, his native servant, all served to evoke the fitness of the British for their imperial mission to conquer and civilise the world. The 'British' aspect of this was important, because until the Act of Union of 1707, the relationship between England and Scotland, Wales and Ireland was by no means seen as one of inevitable union. As late as the 1690s, Scottish entrepreneurs were pursuing an exclusively Scottish mercantilist overseas enterprise, namely the Company of Scotland's scheme to establish its own commercial entrepot at Darien, on the Isthmus of Panama.[16] The Act of Union aimed in part to scupper the Darien scheme and with it any prospect of an independent Celtic imperial project. Even after the Act of Union, sporadic upsurges of Scottish resistance to London's rule, meant that the establishment of a British identity could not be regarded as a *fait accompli*; it had to be promoted and nurtured, by incorporating Scottish Lairds into the ruling elite of the United Kingdom and its empire, and by· popular celebrations of Britishness.[17] In part the latter was achieved by emphasising the (partial) Protestant unity of the British as distinct from the Catholicism of the continental powers; as well as other unifying factors such as the monarchy and language. Global conflicts and the British empire in particular offered a collective project in which all members of the United Kingdom could participate and celebrate. In this way the imperial ideal and its mercantilist philosophy provided the mortar to bind together the fortress which was the new United Kingdom. The lyrics of Thomas Arne's *Rule Britannia*, written at the height of British imperial warfare in the middle of the century, extolled the Britons as masters of the oceans by divine right in as ardent a piece of imperial British bombast as ever penned.

Yet in spite of this institutional entrenchment of imperialist ideas, and the urgent priorities of intermittent global conflict, towards the end of the eighteenth century mercantilism began to be seriously challenged. On the intellectual front, there had always been dissenting voices about empire and aspects of mercantilist thinking. David Hume (1711–76), born to a prosperous Scottish family, was a fierce advocate of the Enlightenment, the intellectual movement which saw human reason as the key to solving the ills of the world and improving the state of humanity. As a philosopher, his controversial views on religion cast him in the role of outsider early in his career. He was refused chairs at the Universities of Edinburgh in 1744/5, and Glasgow in 1751/2 through the influence of highly placed critics. Deeply sceptical about the supposed benefits of empire, Hume also challenged the intellectual foundations of mercantilism.[18] Although his position as something of an outcast cost Hume dear in terms of his academic career, it also freed him to give full rein and voice to his rationalist beliefs.

He contended in the 1750s that the 'balance of trade' argument in favour of colonies, to secure supplies of essential goods without this being accompanied by a damaging outflow of treasure, was based on a fallacious misunderstanding of both the nature of wealth and the effects of large imports of bullion upon a national economy. Hume argued that mercantilists confused wealth with money – for Hume the wealth of a nation was determined by the total value of the commodities contained therein, not the stock of money. Greedy accumulation of bullion would not enrich the nation, but merely increase the quantity of money pursuing the same fixed volume of goods for sale, resulting in inflation, and a diminution of the nation's exports as its produce was priced out of the international market.[19] But it was Adam Smith's *Wealth of Nations* which launched the most devastating assault on mercantilist orthodoxy.

A friend of Hume and, like him, a Scot, Smith (1723–90) eventually emerged as an even more formidable champion of the Enlightenment. He avoided the controversy which surrounded Hume's career however, and became first Professor of Logic, then Moral Philosophy at the University of Glasgow in 1751–52. His reputation as a teacher and thinker won him considerable renown, and when he moved to London in 1776, he found himself placed among the intellectual elite of his day, including such men as Samuel Johnson and Benjamin Franklin. The publication of *Wealth of Nations* in 1776 came at a time when industrialisation and the flourishing of a modern market economy were taking root in Britain, and made an immediate impact. Trouble in the American colonies was also rapidly escalating into full-scale war, which lent Smith's analysis of empire even greater purchase on the contemporary intellectual community. Smith was particularly critical of the protectionist tendencies of mercantilism.[20] He reiterated Hume's critique of mercantilism's incomprehension of the nature of wealth and its fixation with accumulating treasure. Much of Smith's analysis of mercantilist principles focused on the American colonies, where the emergent independence movement lent his criticisms added weight. His conclusions were controversial and uncompromising. Smith argued that possession of the American colonies contributed nothing to enhance the wealth of Britain. This was because the colonial monopolies had the effect of artificially inflating the profitability of these branches of trade, thereby drawing capital away from domestic, non-monopolistic fields of commerce. The effect on the domestic British economy was therefore to stifle truly competitive enterprise. Because fewer entrepreneurs were choosing to invest in domestic spheres of production, competition therein diminished. The higher prices of British products which resulted made them less competitive in the international market. Overall, monopolies misallocated resources, because they prevented the market from achieving the most efficient use of capital and labour, an outcome which could only result from free competition. Monopolies therefore undermined national prosperity. Smith believed that the best way to promote economic success was by allowing the 'hidden hand' of the market to operate through free trade and minimal state interference. Capital would thereby be forced to find the most profitable and productive lines of investment available. Human ingenuity and the uneven distribution of natural resources would promote increasingly sophisticated innovations in production involving the more effective use of skill and resources through an elaborate national and international division of labour. Smith believed that the most remunerative of the new fields of investment would be domestic ones, since returns from agriculture and manufacturing at home would be more rapid and reliable than overseas investment, where greater risk and distance meant a longer waiting time for maturation of interests. Smith believed that surplus capital would inevitably arise, especially in small countries like Britain, and that this would naturally find its way into either foreign trade or investment in overseas ventures such as plantation agriculture. But the implication was that overseas trade would be somewhat marginal in the scheme of national economy. The advantage of this would be to curb the friction which international trade generated between the European powers, since its perceived relative importance in the accumulation of national wealth would be diminished. In this sense, Smith believed that mercantilism artificially inflated the significance of foreign trade in international relations. Smith argued for a gradual relaxation of colonial trade monopolies, together with the dismantling of the privileges enjoyed by the various companies and interest groups which had benefited from mercantilist strategies in the past. Significantly however, he stopped short of recommending a complete demolition of the imperial mercantilist edifice. He was surprisingly hesitant on the question of decolonisation, conceding that colonies did, in certain circumstances, enhance the national interest. He also strongly supported those aspects of the Navigation Acts which secured for Britain a strong maritime system of defence. It was an ambivalence about empire which was to reappear in the writings of many later liberal commentators.

Smith's nostrums on mercantilism, free trade and empire caught the winds of social change in Britain. The eighteenth century saw unprecedented economic growth, as land enclosure and the beginnings of industrialisation launched the long process of economic modernisation. Associated with these developments was the growth of the market economy, and new economic interest groups – industrialists, traders and others, who were hungry for new markets at home and abroad, and who were increasingly frustrated at the protectionism and monopolistic privileges enjoyed by established interests under the mercantilist system. As a result, intellectual advocates of free trade like Smith found their ideas being championed by new political pressure groups campaigning for economic liberalisation. The main thrust of these ideas was not centrally concerned with empire and colonies, but they inevitably implied changing policies towards empire. From the 1790s, successive governments felt a mounting wave of political campaigns for economic change. Initially these consisted mainly of attacks upon the trading privileges of the East India Company, whose monopoly of trade was unsuccessfully challenged by pro-free trade groups in the debate leading to the renewal of the company's charter in 1793.[21] But during the Napoleonic wars, support for these ideas gathered momentum, with the East India Company being dislodged from its India trade monopoly in 1813 by a combination of London and provincial free trade interests.[22]

By the post-war period laissez-faire liberal ideology was gathering greater intellectual credibility as well as political support, as new thinkers developed Smith's ideas. David Ricardo's work on the emergent international division of labour, and the comparative advantages which nations with different climates and natural resources would accrue from the specialisation which free trade made possible, strengthened the hand of the free traders.[23] Just as the writings of Mun and Child had represented the views of those directly involved in running mercantilist enterprise, so David Ricardo (1772–1823) spoke for those engaged in the emerging system of free trade capitalism. The son of Jewish refugees from Holland, Ricardo built a spectacularly successful career as a dealer on the London Stock Exchange, retiring a rich man at the age of forty two. He served as an MP from 1819 until his death, and offered his expertise in debates about various economic controversies of the day, including the question of the Gold Standard. His commercial and political careers provided insights into domestic and international commerce which enabled him to build upon the work of Adam Smith, whose work had been enormously influential over Ricardo. Other intellectuals added weight to the new ideas on trade and commerce. Malthus, Bentham and John Stuart Mill all asserted the validity of the new liberal, laissez-faire economic ideology. Inexorably, the new political economy won the day. Between 1815 and 1850, pillar after pillar of protectionism and mercantilism were brought crashing down. In 1833, the East India Company lost its remaining trading monopoly to China. Thirteen years later the Corn Laws were repealed following years of dogged campaigning by the Manchester-led Anti-Corn Law League; and in 1849 even the Navigation Acts were abolished. By 1850, mercantilist protectionism was dead, and free trade had become the orthodoxy of the day. Government economic policy in other fields were progressively dictated by liberal ideology, with a growing emphasis upon the Gold Standard, balanced budgets, minimum state intervention in the economy and low taxation.

In respect of the empire however, as opposed to mercantilism, the legacy of this economic revolution was more complex. Superficially, laissez-faire ideology was distinctly hostile to empire on several grounds. If free trade could deliver the wants and needs of the nation, why incur the cost and danger of colonies? Expense was no small consideration. Colonial frontiers had to be defended, and presented additional dangers of war. The new political economy dictated that public expenditure and taxation be kept to a minimum, to maximise the financial incentives for entrepreneurship. Empire building brought with it unpredictable military costs and a heightened risk of international conflict. Certainly some adherents of the new philosophy subscribed to this view. In his early writings, Jeremy Bentham (1748–1832) was even more doubtful of the importance of foreign trade than Smith, arguing, in accordance with Say's Law, that the purchasing power generated by a nation's production was sufficient to ensure a market for its output. This led Bentham to reject both the need for colonies and even the Navigation Acts, since overseas commerce was of limited importance.[24] Bentham even tried to set out a scheme for a new system of diplomacy, which would facilitate multilateral decolonisation and usher in a new phase of international harmony.[25] Later in the mid-Victorian period, some mainstream Liberal politicians took up this free market, anti-imperial line. Probably the most outspoken was Richard Cobden (1804–65), who in the 1840s and 1850s became the fiercest parliamentary critic of empire. Cobden was the son of an unsuccessful farmer who overcame poverty to establish himself by the early 1830s as a prosperous textile manufacturer in Manchester. He was elected MP for Stockport in 1841, but was already an ardent champion of free trade and the emerging class of industrial entrepreneurs. Cobden's early hardship, and his success as a self-made businessman, imbued him with a deep resentment of hereditary power and privilege. To him imperialism represented the worst of the aristocratic and militaristic vested interests who had dominated British political life for too long. A fervent opponent of most British military adventures overseas, including the Crimean War, he especially damned those resulting in imperial conquest. He strongly condemned Britain's second war against Burma in 1851, which ended with the annexation of the remaining coastal region of the state.[26] Cobden aspired to an international regime of free trade, which he believed would encourage interdependence and peace, and render war impractical, self-defeating and obsolete. Cobden's influence within the emergent Liberal Party was considerable, and his conviction of the incompatibility of empire and sound economic policy struck a chord with a generation of his political peers. Given the Liberal Party's dominance of government between 1846 and 1874, Cobdenism seemed to exercise national as well as party political leverage. In addition, the inconsistency of liberty and widening enfranchisement at home, and despotic authoritarianism in the empire, sat uneasily on the consciences of late nineteenth-century Liberals like Gladstone, who at least expressed disquiet at British imperialism even if he did not usually act upon it.

But running counter to this anti-imperialist strand of liberal thought was one which sought to reconcile colonialism with economic liberal ideas, out of a deepening sense of unease about the social and economic consequences of industrialisation for British society. By the 1820s, the deleterious social effects of industrialisation were becoming all too evident in the squalor of Britain's burgeoning towns and cities, while sporadic explosions of industrial conflict and political dissent alarmed those for whom the French Revolution was an uncomfortably recent memory. Added to this, the gloomy predictions by Thomas Malthus (1766–1834) of an inevitable catastrophe caused by growth in population outstripping the global capacity for food production, helped create a profound sense of foreboding in the minds of even the most enthusiastic adherent of laissez faire.[27] Crime, poverty, the prospect of widespread starvation and social collapse in Britain led many to conclude that empire did, after all, have a place in their scheme for the world. Early analysts of British society such as Patrick Colquhoun were quick to use Malthusian arguments in favour of colonies as an outlet for surplus population.[28] In the 1830s, a wayward ex-convict and commercial adventurer, Edward Gibbon Wakefield (1796–1862) set up the National Colonisation Society to promote the settlement of British subjects in those newly acquired imperial possessions overseas with an abundance of land. His involvement in the colonisation of New Zealand is well recorded, but more important was his argument in favour of colonisation as a way of finding a vent for Britain's surplus population and capital.[29] Wakefield's ideas appealed to contemporary social and political anxieties, but to some extent the principle was not new. The British had already been dumping their convict population in Australia for several decades. What was different about Wakefield's argument was his espousal of a planned programme of colonisation, involving careful allocation of land to settlers, the conscious export of British culture, and the establishment of strong ties with the mother country. Because settlers would, in effect, possess all the attributes of true-born Britons, so it followed that they would speedily progress to self government, albeit under the umbrella of the empire. Here was a carefully argued defence of imperialisim, which appealed both to economic reasoning and patriotism. Colonial settlement became a principal justification of empire espoused by the British elite – even among those of a liberal persuasion. As the nineteenth century unfolded, the granting of a strong measure of self government first to Canada, then later to New Zealand and Australia, went some way to soothing the moral qualms of those worried by the undemocratic character of imperialism. Ideologically, it seemed that 'responsible' self government for these colonies allowed liberals to have their imperial cake and eat it.

Thus it was that, regardless of the misgivings of the anti-imperial faction of the Liberal party, the British empire continued to expand, even during the supposedly anti-imperialist high noon of Liberal dominance in the mid-nineteenth century. As Gallagher and Robinson point out, between 1851 and 1871, New Zealand, the Gold Coast, Sind, the Punjab, Hong Kong, Berar, Awadh, Lower Burma, Lagos and a large slice of southern Africa were all incorporated into the empire.[30] According to them this was merely the tip of a large imperial iceberg, which also included large swathes of the earth's surface over which the British enjoyed informal influence. In the last thirty years of the century, the pace of expansion quickened. By 1900, much of Africa had been conquered, including Egypt, the Sudan, Rhodesia (modern Zimbabwe), and what would become Uganda and Kenya. In the south of the continent Britain was on the brink of war to swallow up the Boer republics, while in south east Asia, the Malay peninsula, Burma and much of northern Borneo were all securely in British hands. Many observers were convinced that large portions of China would follow. Of course, the British were not alone in scrambling for colonies. France, Germany, Russia, as well as some of the lesser European powers such as Belgium and Holland, had all extended their empires; indeed competition between them had been a factor driving on this latest phase of imperial expansion. By the time of Queen Victoria's death in 1901, the British empire was openly celebrated as the largest and mightiest in history. It seemed to some that the zenith of imperial power had been achieved.

Unsurprisingly this new wave of imperial acquisitions was accompanied, and to some extent promoted, by new estimations of the value of empire. Indeed, the late Victorian period saw an intensification of the debate between imperial enthusiasts and sceptics. As one recent historian has demonstrated, there was always an inconsistency between the smallness of Britain and its resources, and the vastness of the empire, a fact not lost on many Victorian analysts.[31] One such contributor was Charles Dilke (1843–1911), a prominent Liberal politician who set out his views in his book *Greater Britain*, published at the beginning of the 1870s. Dilke came from the radical wing of the party, and his travels as a young man through Australia, New Zealand, Canada and the USA convinced him that the common cultural and racial heritage of the Anglo-Saxon peoples who dominated these emergent nations would shape the future development of international economic and political relations. Dilke predicted that British power would inevitably wane as other developing nations (especially the USA) began to make their superior natural resources tell in economic competition and international relations. He argued, however, that in practice this was of little importance because the USA, as a former British colony, shared a powerful sense of affinity with the rest of the Anglo-Saxon world created by the British empire.[32] Dilke urged his countrymen to accept the eventual independence of the colonies, particularly those parts of the 'white empire' like Australia, New Zealand and Canada which already enjoyed a high degree of self government. More important was that the British economy should continue to prosper, because only this would ensure the well-being and stability of the nation; and here Dilke subscribed to the classical economic prescription of laissez faire, free trade and balanced budgets, policies which were all hampered by the costs and consequences of empire. There was always a strong body of opinion within the Liberal Party which subscribed to this view, and occasionally the leadership seemed to espouse it vigorously. In the late 1870s, for example, Gladstone's famous 'Midlothian campaign' against the aggressively imperialist overtones of Conservative foreign policy in the near east, echoed many of these sentiments, though the subsequent Liberal administration could not resist an even greater adventure of their own in the conquest of Egypt.

By the 1870s, however, imperialism was finding more resolute political and intellectual defenders. The Conservative Party of Disraeli was redefining itself in ways that would broaden its electoral appeal to the middle classes and the recently enfranchised section of the working class. Disraeli claimed that Conservatism stood for the interests of all classes, for the nation at large, and an important component of this national appeal was the defence and celebration of the British empire. Disraeli's speech at the Crystal Palace in June 1872 boldly contrasted the Conservative commitment 'to uphold the Empire of England' with the efforts by successive Liberal administrations 'to effect the disintegration of the Empire of England'.[33] Even though in practice Tory policy towards empire was as cautious as the Liberals, Disraeli had cast the future of empire into the cauldron of political debate.

Disraeli's defence of empire gathered strong intellectual support from some quarters in the 1870s, not least from one of the most eminent historians of the day, J. A. Froude (1818–94).[34] James Anthony Froude, son of an Archdeacon of Totnes, emerged as a prominent Oxford historian in the 1840s. Ordained deacon at the age of twenty seven in 1845, with his brother Richard Hurrell Froude, J. A. Froude became deeply involved in the Oxford Movement, which sought to stress the continuity with earlier Christian traditions in the teachings of the Church of England. It sought to assert the legitimacy of England's post-Reformation national church, to stress some of its common elements with Roman Catholicism, and revive faith in it as a valid source of religious truth. From this perspective, Froude's historical interests were inexorably drawn to the origins of the Reformation, particularly the reign of Henry VIII. Froude concluded that the English monarchy and society were unique, not only in the peculiar virtues of their national church, but also in spreading their national values and beliefs across the world through empire and colonisation. Although Froude later broke with the Oxford Movement, his belief in the inherent moral superiority of traditional English society was reinforced by his close connection with Thomas Carlyle (1795–1881), whose academic influence lent weight to Froude's admiration for traditional order and strong government. It followed that Froude had a dim view of those at home or in the colonies who rejected the authority of the crown, the aristocracy, the Church of England, and the traditional system of values associated with those institutions. By the time Froude wrote about the British empire in the 1870s, he was Rector of St Andrews University, and already enjoyed a national reputation. His close association with the Conservative Party's pro-imperial stance was underlined in 1874, when the new Tory Colonial Secretary Lord Carnarvon sent Froude to South Africa to report on the most effective way to secure federation of the various British and Dutch colonies and states.

Largely because of its successful rebellion against British rule in the eighteenth century, the USA was deeply distrusted by Froude. He regarded its democratic culture as profoundly inimical to British interests and social values of hierarchy, duty and noblesse oblige. To accept passively the displacement of British global hegemony by the Americans was to Froude the utmost folly, undermining the beneficial influence around the world of the traditional British way of life. Suspicious of the democratising and urbanising tendencies of industrialisation in Britain itself, Froude regarded the colonies of settlement as the last bastion of traditional British values. He argued therefore for a policy of promoting British emigration to the white empire, whilst simultaneously strengthening the bonds between them and the mother country. As Britain's modernisation swept away the old rural society and the virtues it embodied, so those attributes would be preserved in Britain's extensive white empire.

Over a decade later another historian further developed Froude's argument, and stimulated the first of several political movements to consolidate and strengthen the empire. J. R. Seeley's *The Expansion of England*, published in 1883, sold over half a million copies by the end of the decade.[35] Sir John Robert Seeley (1834–95) was the son of a publisher and religious writer. Educated at Cambridge, his background was in classics, but the success of his religious work *Ecce Homo* on the life and teachings of Christ, led (rather curiously) in 1869 to his appointment as Regius Professor of Modern History at Cambridge. As a historian, Seeley's early works were indifferently received. His *The Life and Times of Stein, or Germany and Prussia in the Napoleonic Wars* (1878) did not achieve great acclaim, though it does provide some insights into Seeley's developing perspective on British imperialism. The sub-text of the book was Seeley's strong British nationalism, and his bitter loathing of Napoleon's project to create a universal European state. Such concerns were not merely abstract historical preoccupations. The 1870s and 1880s were a time of deepening European tension, with the rise of a unified Germany and its system of alliances with Austria-Hungary and Italy. The prospect of another major European war undoubtedly shaped Seeley's consideration of the British empire and its future. Neither could Seeley ignore the emergence of the USA as a huge economic power and potential future empire. For Seeley, the value of history lay in its capacity to illuminate and inform current political issues, as his musings on the British empire in many ways epitomised. The future of Britain, whose smallness and finite resources seemed in danger of being dwarfed in a new world of great continental powers and alliances, was the latent question underlying a series of lectures given by Seeley at Cambridge in 1881 and 1882 on the British empire. These formed the basis of *The Expansion of England*, which won Seeley a lasting reputation and eventually a knighthood before his death in 1895.

Famous for his view that the British acquired their empire in a fit of absence of mind, Seeley argued that the British empire represented the creation of a 'Greater Britain', meaning the establishment of a transcontinental political, ethnic and cultural community of the English speaking peoples. Seeley contended that the future of this community lay in ever strengthening ties between the separate elements, through a system of imperial federation. While the USA had withdrawn from this community, the white empire remained large enough for it to establish a unified 'Greater Britain' able to match emergent super states such as the USA and the Russian empire in manpower and resources. Seeley believed that the emergence of large, resource-rich superpowers was an inevitable consequence of the industrial age, and he recognised that a small country like Britain had no chance to retain its position as a first-class power without enhancing its resources and population through the permanent consolidation of its empire. While Seeley readily conceded the ethnic and cultural affinity which existed between the British and the Americans, for him political sovereignty lay at the core of political power, and that required the maintenance and strengthening of the British empire as a distinct and separate political entity. Imperial federation of the empire, effectively its consolidation as 'super state', would enable the British to retain their position of global influence.

Seeley's work generated a political response. In 1884 the Imperial Federation League (IFL) was established to promote the consolidation of commercial, military and political bonds between the component parts of the empire. While the IFL ultimately broke up in 1893, its ideas had a real impact. In 1887 the first of several Colonial Conferences were held by the British government with a view to securing closer co-operation within the empire in the military and economic spheres. Furthermore, the emergence of pro-imperial sentiment from the 1870s threw up a new generation of politicians who were receptive to ideas of imperial consolidation. By the 1890s, even the Liberal Party, traditionally the home of imperial scepticism, boasted a faction who styled themselves as 'Liberal Imperialists'. Within the Unionist camp, the most dynamic pro-imperial figure to emerge was Joseph Chamberlain (1836–1914), the brilliant but maverick Birmingham politician. As Colonial Secretary in the late 1890s, Chamberlain proved an aggressive proponent of empire, and his role in bringing about the Boer War of 1899–1902 is well recorded. By then, the question of imperial unity had acquired greater urgency. The perceived 'great depression' of the 1880s, the growing American and German challenge to British economic dominance in the markets of the world, and sharpening global tensions following the scramble for colonies and the emergence of the rival European military alliances, all served to plunge the British political establishment into a crisis of confidence. By the beginning of the twentieth century, empire was becoming central to policy questions about economic and military strength. Probably the most important manifestation of this was the emergence of Chamberlain's Tariff Reform League in 1903, an organisation committed to closer economic and political union within the empire, as a strategy for preserving British power in the new age of emergent super-powers. As a result, the beginning of the new century saw fresh attempts to assess the meaning and significance of empire, several of which drew upon the new intellectual currents in economics and the other social sciences to provide new perspectives. The next chapter will chart the development of what came to be known generally as the economic interpretation of British imperialism.

Notes

1 D. Armitage, *The Ideological Origins of the British Empire* (Cambridge, 2000).
2 *Ibid.*, pp. 28–9.
3 *Ibid.*, pp. 163–5.
4 L. Colley, *Captives: Britain, Empire and the World 1600–1850* (London, 2003), p. 155.
5 P. J. Marshall (ed.), *The Oxford History of the British Empire* Vol 2 (Oxford, 1998), introduction p. 2.
6 R. B. Sheridan, 'The formation of Caribbean plantation society, 1689–1748', in P. J. Marshall (ed.), *The Oxford History of the British Empire*, Vol. 2, pp. 394–414, p. 400.
7 C. A. Bayly, 'The first age of global imperialism c. 1760–1830', *Journal of Imperial and Commonwealth History* 26:2 (1998), 28–47.
8 Colley, *Captives*, p. 200.
9 See Armitage, *The Ideological Origins of the British Empire*, pp. 70–81.
10 S. Purchas, *Hakluytus Posthumus or Purchas his Pilgrimes* (London, 1625).
11 Armitage, *The Ideological Origins of the British Empire*, pp. 97–8.
12 See K. E. Knorr, *British Colonial Theories 1570–1850* (Toronto, 1944), pp. 12–13.

13 *Ibid.*, pp. 85–7.

14 P. Lawson, *The East India Company: A History* (London, 1993), pp. 19–20.

15 P. J. Cain and A. G. Hopkins, *British Imperialism*, pp. 76–80.

16 Armitage, *The Ideological Origins of the British Empire*, pp. 159–61.

17 C. A. Bayly, *Imperial Meridian: The British Empire and the World 1780–1830* (London, 1989), pp. 81–9; L. Colley, *Britons: Forging the Nation 1707–1837* (London, 1996), pp. 1–9.

18 See Armitage, *The Ideological Origins of the British Empire*, pp. 188–94.

19 Knorr, *British Colonial Theories*, p. 156.

20 A. Smith, *An Inquiry into the Nature and Causes of the Wealth of Nations* (London, 1961 edn.).

21 A. Tripathi, *Trade and Finance in the Bengal Presidency 1793–1833* (Calcutta, 1979), pp. 21–6.

22 A. Webster, 'The political economy of trade liberalization: the East India Company Charter Act of 1813', *Economic History Review* 13:3 (1990), 404–19.

23 See D. Ricardo, *On the Principles of Political Economy and Taxation* (London, 1821).

24 J. Bentham, 'Colonies and navy', in W. Stark (ed.), *Economic Writings of Jeremy Bentham*, Vol. 2 (London, 1952), pp. 211–18; see also D. Winch, *Classical Political Economy and Colonies* (London, 1965).

25 J. Bentham, *A Plan for an Universal and Perpetual Peace* (London, 1939).

26 R. Cobden, *How Wars are Got up in India: The Origin of the Burmese War* (London, 1853).

27 T. Malthus, *An Essay on the Principle of Population as it Affects the Future Improvement on Society* (London, 1996 edn.).

28 P. Colquhoun, *A Treatise on the Wealth, Power and Resources of the British Empire* (London, 1814).

29 See E. G. Wakefield, *England and America: A Comparison of the Social and Political State of Both Nations* (London, 1833), 2 vols; E. G. Wakefield, *A View of the Art of Colonisation in Present Reference to the British Empire in Letters between a Statesman and a Colonist* (London, 1849).

30 Gallagher and Robinson, 'The imperialism of free trade', p. 2.

31 Colley, *Captives*, pp. 370–2.

32 C. Dilke, 'Greater Britain', in P. J. Cain (ed.), *Empire and Imperialism: The Debate of the 1870s*, pp. 20–6.

33 Disraeli's speech at the Crystal Palace 24 June 1872, P. Adelman, *Gladstone, Disraeli and Later Victorian Politics* (London, 1983), pp. 83–4.

34 J. A. Froude, 'England and her colonies' (1872) in Cain (ed.) *Empire and Imperialism*, pp. 27–49.

35 J. R. Seeley, *The Expansion of England* (London, 1883); see also E. H. H. Green, 'The political economy of empire 1880–1914', in A. Porter (ed.), *The Oxford History of the British Empire: Vol. 3 The Nineteenth Century* (Oxford, 1999), pp. 346–70.

3

Capitalism's critics and defenders: early twentieth-century economic explanations of Victorian British imperial expansion

If most explanations of British imperialism in the age of expansion were triumphant or justificatory in tone, the onset of doubts and difficulty at the end of the nineteenth century set the scene for more pessimistic assessments of British imperialism, which looked to political economy rather than theories of national development or race to explain the causes and consequences of empire. While the flourishing of the social sciences in the latter years of the century, especially sociology and economics, contributed significantly to this approach, it was the onset of a collective loss of confidence in Britain's position in the world which was the real stimulus. The emergence of Germany and the USA as major industrial competitors challenged Britain's once seemingly unassailable reputation as the 'workshop of the world'. Politicians, academics and intellectuals poured forth an expansive literature seeking to explain and postulate remedies for this unwelcome development. Writers such as E. E. Williams, F. A. Mackenzie and A. Shadwell bemoaned what they saw as deteriorating British industrial efficiency in the face of burgeoning foreign growth.[1] Karl Pearson and Benjamin Kidd offered a more sinister assessment of this intensified international competition based on ideas of racial competition and eugenics.[2] The outbreak and faltering progress of the Boer war (1899–1902) heightened this concern, as the Boers achieved stunning early victories, British casualties mounted, and large numbers of potential recruits were turned away because of their poor physical condition. The latter confirmed the groundbreaking social research of Rowntree and Booth, which demonstrated the alarming extent of poverty in Britain.[3] These developments elicited a serious response from politicians and intellectuals across the political spectrum, and the issue of 'national efficiency' became the subject of intense political and academic debate.[4] The two emergent political movements of New Liberalism and the Tariff Reform League (from 1903) both emphasised the need for social reforms, the former advocating redistributive taxation and the latter income from import tariffs to pay for them. New worries about Anglo-German naval rivalry after 1900 kept fears about national efficiency at the top of the agenda, and defined the key priorities of the Liberal governments of 1906 to 1914: welfare reforms and military expansion.

It was inevitable that this debate would turn to the question of the British empire. Joseph Chamberlain's Tariff Reform League envisaged it as the saviour of British fortunes at a time when the vast resources of the USA and Russia seemed to promise one of them future hegemony. An imperial federation, in which a common external tariff protected domestic economies from foreign competition, and strengthened the economic ties which bound the empire together, would ensure the lasting presence on the world stage of the British and her 'offspring'.[5] But even at the time of its conception this idea carried little weight in Britain's white dominions, which were already looking to greater political and economic independence from the mother country. Several consecutive electoral defeats would ensure that imperial preference would be only a brief experiment during the First World War, and later a more protracted response to the ravages of the world depression of the 1930s. But by then the idea of true imperial federation was no longer a credible option.

In contrast with the pro-imperial stance of the Chamberlainites there emerged a deeply critical analysis of empire from a supporter of New Liberalism, the sophistication and erudition of which was to ensure its relevance to the present day. The prime mover of this interpretation was a journalist, John Atkinson Hobson (1858–1940), whose prolific writings on imperialism were to establish him as the principal theorist of the rise of the late nineteenth century British empire, the 'New Imperialism' of the post 1870 period. The son of a Derby newspaper proprietor, Hobson overcame early academic disappointment to build a distinguished career as a writer and intellectual. His fascination with national politics led him to become first a committed Liberal, and later a member of the Labour party, in the wake of the wartime disintegration of the Liberals. This political dimension had a profound bearing upon his writing, which covered a vast range of topics, and which frequently took partisan positions in defence of his political affiliations. Among these, Hobson became best known for his publications on the question of imperialism.

In many ways, Hobson embodied much of the controversy surrounding the question of the British empire. Most accounts of Hobson's work present it as a coherent and consistent theory of empire, an unchanging statement of one particular view.[6] This assessment is based mainly on a reading of Hobson's principal work on empire, *Imperialism: A Study*, published in 1902.[7] But a recent study of its author by Peter Cain paints a more complex picture of Hobson, in which his views were changeable and contradictory, shifting with the impact of events and as the author revisited his work.[8] As Cain demonstrates, this volatility partly reflected Hobson's sometimes undisciplined approach to his subject, and his role as an active and partisan political commentator. But one also detects a universal uncertainty about both the driving force behind and the global legacy of empire which must have been experienced by all writers on this complex subject. Cain shows, for example, that Hobson's negative assessment of the effects of overseas investment on British society in *Imperialism*, gave way to a much more positive evaluation in *An Economic Interpretation of Investment* published in 1911.[9] However, the onset of world war in 1914, and the return of international tensions in the late 1930s, compelled Hobson to swing back towards his views outlined in *Imperialism*, though there was some oscillation between his 'pro' and 'anti' stances on foreign investment during this period.[10] *Imperialism*, which was reprinted in 1905 and in 1938 shortly before his death, probably did represent the balance of his opinion over his lifetime, though the pendulum swing of his views is significant in itself, indicating both the complexity of the subject and the trajectory of Hobson's own political and personal development. Cain makes the point that before the First World War, the book enjoyed limited popularity, even in Liberal circles, but in the 1930s the deterioration of international relations and the rise of Japanese, German and Italian imperial ambitions breathed new life into Hobson's study of imperial rivalry, and paved the way for a further reprint.[11] This edition was reprinted again in 1988 for an academic market. Together with several other publications, *Imperialism* provides the basis for the interpretation of Hobson presented here.[12]

Hobson's ideas on empire, like his political philosophy in general, were shaped profoundly by his background and life experiences. His devout Liberalism reflected a long-standing family loyalty to the party, expressed staunchly by his father, William, the proprietor of the *Derbyshire Advertiser and Journal*. The family's was a distinctly provincial version of Liberalism, which celebrated the rugged, individual industrialist as the embodiment of social and political virtue. Effete aristocrats and money grubbing metropolitan financiers were condemned for their alleged corruption, privilege and self interested opposition to free trade and all its benefits. Unsurprisingly, Hobson's political hero was Richard Cobden, the Manchester School critic of imperialism and champion of the small businessman. Cobdenite principles ultimately led Hobson to the conclusion that imperialism was the product of the selfish collusion between a corrupt aristocratic state and unscrupulous metropolitan business interests, whose greed and disregard for the interests of both the impoverished masses and the nation at large, were the driving force behind overseas conquest. But while Hobson implicated British capitalism in the late Victorian scramble for colonies, his main target was metropolitan finance rather than provincial industry. In this respect, Hobson's was the perspective of the provincial middle class outsider, which condemned the overweening wealth and power of London capital but took care to distinguish it from the more acceptable face of industrial capitalism outside the home counties. A sense of exclusion from the privileged inner circle of status and power is almost palpable in Hobson's writings, as is indignation at the displacement from the centre of the political order of the provincial industrialists in favour of the City money men. In part this may have reflected Hobson's own feelings of rejection from the academic world after personal circumstances thwarted his aspirations in that direction, but other aspects of his experience were probably more formative. As an active journalist in southern Africa Hobson witnessed the ugly realities of empire at the sharp end. As a political activist he was swept along by the revolution in Liberal thinking at the beginning of the twentieth century. New Liberalism was a response to various perceived ills in British society. These included the apparent deterioration of the country's position in the world as Germany and the USA cut down Britain's economic lead, and the fear that widespread poverty would not only accelerate that decline, but also foment political revolution. The rise of organised labour and increasingly bitter industrial conflict heightened this growing sense of national crisis. In addition, as a staunch Cobdenite advocate of a world order of peace and free commerce, Hobson could only be deeply alarmed by the colonial and military rivalries between the great powers, and the global conflagration they threatened. Hobson managed to weave these contemporary ideas and concerns into a new and coherent analysis of the late Victorian 'age of imperialism'.

At the heart of Hobson's explanation of British imperial expansion in the later nineteenth century was an analysis of British domestic social development during that period. Like other contemporary observers, Hobson was deeply concerned by the unequal distribution of wealth within the British population, the contrast of a huge concentration of wealth among the upper ranks with grinding poverty for the mass of the working class. Capitalist development in Britain had taken an unfortunate turn in amassing too much wealth and power into too few hands, in the form of large industrial firms, and even more formidably wealthy merchant banks and other financial institutions. Hobson hankered after a theoretical earlier stage of capitalism, found more in the writings of Adam Smith rather than in reality, in which smaller firms and a more pristine competitive environment fashioned a less unequal society.[13] The root of imperial expansion lay in the inability of the impoverished masses to pay for and consume the expanding volume of produce issuing forth from Britain's industries. Because there was a limit on the ability and inclination of the rich to consume this produce, British industrial-ists were increasingly compelled to seek foreign markets for their goods. This in itself contributed to imperial expansion, as British exporters sought to protect overseas markets from competitors, but it was not the main motivation behind imperialism. Exporters, after all, could find new markets if existing ones disappeared. It was a second economic interest group, financiers and investors, who Hobson identified as the strongest advocates of empire. The suppression of the domestic market in Britain due to inequality and poverty had resulted in a dearth of investment opportunities, compelling investors and wealthy financiers to look overseas for new openings. Hobson believed that this weakness of the British market (a phenomenon which he called underconsumption) produced an unnaturally high propensity for capital as well goods to be exported. Hobson noted that the interests of overseas investors were much more vulnerable than those of exporters of goods. The industrialist selling in foreign markets might be inconvenienced and harmed in the short run by the sudden closure of foreign markets, but there would usually be no loss of assets, and new markets could always be found. But for foreign investors, their very assets themselves could be placed in danger by adverse developments in the territories or nations where they were located. Funds sunk into a railway or gold mine were not easy to rescue and repatriate. Inevitably therefore, investors placed a high premium on protecting their foreign property. Where these were located in the stable and advanced economies such as the USA, there was generally little cause for concern; but those in the less developed world, where local political structures might be unstable or vulnerable to the incursions of powers hostile to British interests, were a source of real and pressing worry. In these circumstances, investors and financiers frequently found it expedient to persuade the British government to assert imperial rule, in order to ensure a safe and stable environment in which their investments could flourish. It was distortions in the British economy wrought by underconsumption, and the high levels of overseas investment they generated, which were therefore at the root of British imperial expansion after 1870.

For Hobson, the politics of empire in the metropole reflected the centrality of financial and investment interests in imperial expansion. Hobson identified numerous groups who benefited from empire: missionaries seeking a safe environment in which to save souls, the officer classes of the military, chasing promotion and glory in colonial adventures, arms manufacturers eager to equip them, and colonial civil servants pursuing advancement and power. But while all of these contributed to the clamour for imperial expansion, it was a powerful coterie of wealthy and influential financiers in the City of London, supported by hundreds of thousands of investors in the south east of England, who were the leaders of the movement for imperial expansion. Leading financiers frequently enjoyed intimate connections with senior politicians and civil servants, as well as with colonial officials and economic interests on the periphery, advantages which enabled them to manipulate political decisions in favour of imperial conquest. Hobson also emphasised the links between some of the more prominent financiers and the press, which were used to stimulate jingoistic popular support for imperialism, thereby adding to the pressure on government to comply.

An important aspect of Hobson's analysis was this ability of the financiers to conspire for empire, to guide politicians towards their desired aims. He identified numerous examples of expansion in which the financiers had consciously manipulated governments to achieve conquest, particularly the invasion of Egypt in 1882, and the war against the Boers from 1899 to 1902. For Hobson, this combination of personal influence, alliance with other pro-imperial pressure groups and an ability to orchestrate popular opinion, equipped the financiers to secure their objectives. The role of government was almost passive, as the executors of policies defined principally by the City of London and its allies. At the heart of this was Hobson's perception of the distribution of power within British society.[14] Hobson noted that industry and finance in Britain were separate entities, with little progress towards the merger of finance and industrial capital evident in Germany and the USA. Only a small proportion of industrial capital was raised through share flotation in the City, or loans from banks. Moreover, in Hobson's eyes City financiers enjoyed superiority in political influence over the provincial industrialists, partly because of the political advantages already outlined, and also because they effectively represented the interests of a key section of the electorate, the thousands of investors in the south east of England who profited from overseas invest-

ment. Hobson believed that as voters they were crucial to electoral success, and this added to the leverage in favour of financial
interests.[15]

What Hobson offered, therefore, was an interpretation of
British imperialism which focused principally upon metropolitan
and economic interests as the main drivers of expansion. The
reissue of *Imperialism: A Study* during Hobson's own lifetime
ensured it a prominent place in the emerging debate about the
expansion of the British empire, and helped to establish the
notion that the roots of imperial expansion lay in the economic
development of Britain and the other great powers. This stress on
metropolitan economic factors was reinforced by theoretical
explanations of empire from an entirely different ideological
stable. Building on Karl Marx's analysis of capitalism, a new
generation of committed Marxist revolutionaries began to turn
their attention to the relationship between capitalism and imperialism, seeking to explain the international expansion of the
capitalist powers, and its implications for the prospect of workers
revolution. Inevitably, this drew them into certain conclusions
about the causes of British imperialism. To understand these, it is
necessary first to consider Marx's own observations on empire.

Writing in England during the mid- and later nineteenth
century, Karl Marx (1818–83) was an observer of the industrial
revolution and its impact upon the already substantial British
empire. While his comrade Frederick Engels provided insights
into the startling advances in productivity achieved in the cotton
mills of Lancashire, Marx lived in London and was well placed to
follow the business of that great city, which was at once the imperial capital and the financial centre of the world. Marx linked
Britain's economic miracle with the growth of her empire. As
explained below, Marx believed that imperialism was an integral
necessity for capitalist industrial development. Moreover, he
believed that the empire would prove to be an international agent
for the spread of capitalism and industry. In the 1850s Marx
argued, for example, that India would be transformed under
British rule from its pre-industrial economic stagnation into a
modern, vibrant capitalist economy.[16] Thus Marx's writings on
British capitalism and imperialism were the commentary of a
contemporary, at once recording and analysing links between the

two phenomena, but also predicting their long-term outcomes. This perspective was compelling in the sense that Marx offered an engaging eye witness account of the unfolding relationship between capitalism and empire. But it is also incomplete in that Marx did not live to see the long-term results of the processes he described. In this respect, he left an open invitation for later followers of his political philosophy to resume the work on imperialism terminated by his death.

Marx postulated that human social development was essentially driven by changes in the way that wealth was created, and by the distribution of power and control over the means of production.[17] Human ingenuity, coupled with evolving social organisation ensured that new kinds of wealth and production would be the dynamo for historical, social and political change. History progressed through different epochs, in each of which the nature of social, economic and political organisation was determined by the means of producing wealth. In each phase of development, power, status and personal wealth were concentrated in the hands of those who owned the means of producing wealth, while those who possessed only their labour power occupied subordinate positions. Thus in the feudal middle ages, the landowning aristocracy dominated society, while the impoverished peasant masses eked out a meagre existence. The political and ideological structures of society reflected and justified this unequal distribution of power and wealth, with the predominance of the monarch and his nobles legitimised by a religious ideology which claimed divine preordination of the existing order. Implicit in this system – and indeed in all epochs where society was so divided by ownership of the means of production – was conflict between the dominant and subordinate classes, as the former sought to extract the maximum labour power from the latter. The increase in food production facilitated by the stability of feudalism paved the way for a division of labour in which individuals, freed from labour in farming, could focus upon trade and craft production. Over time, this permitted the emergence of a new form of wealth generation, based on manufacturing, market-based relations, urbanisation and progressively more sophisticated technologies of production. But again, society was divided between the emerging capitalists (bourgeoisie) who

owned this new means of production, and their urbanised industrial employees (proletariat) who had to sell their labour. Spurred
on by the need to establish a political system which reflected their
own interests rather than those of the old pre-industrial landed
elite, the capitalists successfully challenged aristocratic hegemony,
and furnished a new political order to meet their own needs; a
process described by Marx as bourgeois revolution.

For Marx the capitalist epoch was the most dynamic phase of
human historical development. Ultimately, the ruthless competition between capitalists, and the relentless development of
labour-saving technologies would inflict mass unemployment and
starvation wages upon the proletariat, whilst their common experience of mass factory production conditions would create a
powerful sense of working-class consciousness and solidarity. The
ultimate outcome would be proletarian revolution and their
establishment of collective, shared ownership of the means of
production. This would represent the end of social divisions and
the beginning of the final epoch of human historical development
leading to communism, in which the huge expansion of wealth-
producing capacity bequeathed by capitalism would be used for
the universal benefit of humankind. Understandably, Marx was
particularly fascinated by the last stages of capitalism, which he
believed were unfolding before his eyes; and he tried to explain
how this process shaped such contemporary phenomena as
European imperial expansion. Marx charted the rapid and
dynamic development of capitalism. In its earliest stages, capitalists were generally small-scale operators employing modest
amounts of capital in relatively simple forms of productive technology, a situation which approximates to the model of 'perfect
competition' presented in classical economics. But the competitive nature of capitalism ensured that this was a fleeting phase. In
the struggle to survive, capitalists were compelled to maximise
their profits in order to reinvest in newer lines of production, and
ever more sophisticated forms of cost-reducing, labour-saving
technology. The result was the elimination of the least efficient
capitalists, and a concentration of capital in the hands of a
decreasing number of larger and richer capitalist firms. The
incentive to constantly gain a competitive edge accelerated the
pace and cost of scientific and technological development,

making entry into the capitalist elite impossible for men without means, and intensifying the need for capitalist organisations to accumulate more capital, and to access other sources of capital, to fund the relentless rounds of new capital investment. The result was reorganisation of capitalist firms to satisfy this hunger for capital; the formation of joint stock public companies which could raise funds by public share issues, and the establishment of ever closer relationships with banks and other financial organisations.

Ultimately, increasing demand for capital investment would have the most deleterious effect on the health of capitalism. As more and more capital was required to sustain a competitive market position, capitalists would find that the rate of return on their investments – the rate of profit – would diminish, eventually to zero. In an effort to stave off this ignominious fate, capitalists resorted to two strategies. The first was to intensify their exploitation of the workforce, paying them less and less for their labour to preserve as much capital as possible. Marx articulated this idea in the form of the labour theory of value, an explanation of the origin of the value of commodities first postulated by the classical economist, David Ricardo.[18] According to this, the value of a commodity was determined by the quantity of labour used to make it. Capitalists accumulated capital by paying their workers less than the value of the labour they used to manufacture the commodities sold by the firm. Capital thus represented 'surplus value', creamed off through the ruthless exploitation of the workforce. One way to prop up the profit rate was to step up this process, but there were limits. Ultimately wages could not be pushed below subsistence level, and as exploitation intensified, so also would worker resistance in the form of strikes and possibly more dangerous forms of militancy. For Marx, of course, herein lay the seeds of revolution and the demise of capitalism.

The second option was to seek out new and cheaper sources of land, raw materials and labour, which could offer at least temporary respite from spiralling costs and diminishing returns. These were, of course, increasingly scarce in those societies already well advanced into the capitalist phase of development, where existing resources and labour supplies had already been thoroughly utilised if not exhausted. They could still be found in abundance in those parts of the world yet to undergo modern capitalist development which, of course, were easy prey to the superior military prowess of the capitalist powers. Though this aspect of the relationship between capitalism and imperialism was not explored in depth by Marx himself, several leading Marxist writers tried to develop this analysis in the early decades of the twentieth century. While their work dealt with the international phenomenon of imperialism rather than the fortunes of any single country, it added a complex dimension to the debate about the origins of the British empire. Unlike Marx, these new Marxist contributors were active revolutionaries, blending their development of Marxist thought with active politics, a combination which undoubtedly coloured their ideas. The two most prominent of these were Rosa Luxemburg (1871–1919), the German revolutionary, and V. I. Lenin (1870–1924), the Russian leader of the Bolshevik Revolution.

Luxemburg outlined her views on the relationship between capitalism and imperialism in her 1913 work, *The Accumulation of Capital*.[19] Born into a middle-class Jewish family in Russian Poland, Luxemburg enjoyed a cosmopolitan education in Poland, Switzerland and France. A revolutionary Marxist from the age of sixteen, Luxemburg won a doctorate in 1898 for her thesis on the industrialisation of her native Poland. She acquired German citizenship by marriage, and from 1898 established herself as a leading figure on the left of the German Social Democratic Party (SPD), the Marxist workers organisation which by 1900 had become the largest left wing party in Europe. She championed the party's commitment to proletarian revolution against Edward Bernstein's advocacy that the SPD abandon that strategy in favour of gradualist reform of capitalism through the parliamentary system. Luxemburg was highly politically active throughout the period leading to the First World War, but her disillusionment with the SPD's acceptance of war in 1914 drove her to break away and form the Spartacus League in 1916, which became the German Communist Party two years later. After spending long periods in prison, her life ended tragically at the hands of ex-soldiers during the post-war revolutionary upheaval in Germany in January 1919.

Luxemburg's work on imperialism was profoundly influenced

by a desire both to reject Bernstein's revisionism and explain the deepening tensions between the European capitalist powers which would shortly lead to the outbreak of war a year after the publication of *The Accumulation of Capital*. The work asserted the irretrievably exploitative and predatory nature of capitalism as a riposte to Bernstein's claims that the system was capable of reform. Luxemburg argued that imperial conquest was essential for the survival of capitalism, and she saw European colonial expansion between 1870 and 1914 as a factor which partly explained the durability of the system in spite of the rise of proletarian organisation and power.

For Luxemburg, the key problem for advanced capitalist societies was the mismatch between the dazzling increase in productive capacity generated by technological advance and the relentless impoverishment of the proletarian masses, driven on by capitalist efforts to prop up the declining profit rate. In the long run the domestic market would be unable to absorb the produce of capitalist industry. In this, Luxemburg came very close to Hobson's own theory of underconsumption. Since other advanced capitalist societies also suffered from the same problem of suppressed domestic economic demand, capitalism would ultimately have to look to the undeveloped world, where capitalism was yet to take root, for new export markets. But here, the predominance of subsistence agriculture as the principal economic activity necessarily limited the immediate size of the market. Primitive agricultural producers living a hand to mouth existence lacked the purchasing power to consume large quantities of industrially produced goods. Thus the conquest of these territories, the export of capital to them, and their initial capitalist development, were all necessary to turn these backwaters into thriving export markets. Only by the creation of market relations and a money economy could self sufficient agrarian producers be transformed into consumers of industrial exports from the advanced capitalist world. Imperialism was thus a device for expanding the markets of capitalism, and temporarily offsetting declining profit rates by spreading the capitalist system to the non-capitalist world. Ultimately, of course, the maturation of these new imperial capitalist economies would bring the same problems which existed in the metropolitan advanced capitalist countries: the reduction of wage levels to subsistence and the concomitant problems of underconsumption and shrinking profit rates. But at least the inevitable would have been staved off for a time. For Luxemburg, imperialism thus seemed to answer the conundrum of why the capitalist system was surviving, in contradiction to Marx's belief a quarter of a century earlier that its demise was probably at hand. In the case of Germany in particular, it offered clues to the inability of Europe's largest Marxist party to deliver revolution, and the emergence of the 'defeatist' revisionist doctrine of Bernstein. Implicit in Luxemburg's thinking was the notion that capitalism could still look forward to quite a long life.

Three years later Lenin offered a different analysis of capitalist development in the age of imperialism. *Imperialism: The Highest Stage of Capitalism* was written at the height of the First World War, and was in part an attempt to explain its origins in the imperialist conflict which was an inevitable consequence of capitalist development.[20] Lenin requires little by way of introduction. The son of a Tsarist civil servant, Vladimir Illyich Ulyanov (his real name) embarked upon a career as a Marxist revolutionary in the 1890s, helping to found the Russian Social Democratic Party. Emerging as the leader of the Bolshevik faction by 1903, Lenin went on to lead the Bolshevik seizure of power in October 1917, and establish the Soviet Union. Lenin was impatient for change, but the limited development of the Tsarist economy, with its overwhelmingly peasant and agricultural nature, made it an unlikely candidate for proletarian revolution. During many years in foreign exile, Lenin gradually adopted the theory of 'permanent revolution' originally devised by Trotsky. This contended that modern capitalism was becoming a progressively international system, in which the economies of nation states were inextricably interlinked by trade and the transnational movement of information and capital. It followed that revolution in one country would so disrupt this delicate system of interdependence that proletarian revolution would sweep across national boundaries like a tidal wave. Thus even semi-feudal nations like Tsarist Russia would proceed rapidly to proletarian revolution. *Imperialism* set out Lenin's justification in terms of Marxist theory for his belief that international revolution was both inevitable and imminent. It has become a classic text of Marxist theory, with endless reprints, especially and unsurprisingly in the countries of the communist bloc. Even after the end of the Cold War, left wing publishers continued to reprint the pamphlet, and in recent years several online versions have appeared.[21] At the end of the twentieth century, academics and polemicists of the left have argued for the continuing relevance of the text in the light of the rise of a globalised economic system.[22]

Lenin picked up where Marx's work ended, in the evolution of capitalism in its latter stages, as firms became fewer, larger and the bourgeoisie fully established its political hegemony within the advanced capitalist nations. Lenin described this stage of mature capitalism as the age of 'monopoly capitalism', the main features of which had been apparent in the more advanced industrial economies since 1900. Monopoly capitalism displayed a number of distinctive features which set it apart from earlier stages of capitalism. Firstly, the ownership of the means of production were concentrated into so few hands that virtual monopolies, or at least tightly controlled oligopolies, had come to dominate the major sectors of production, be they industrial or in the financial services. Lenin cited how industrial cartels and a handful of major banks had come to dominate the economic life of the USA, France and Germany by the early 1900s.[23] The second feature was a merging of industrial and banking capital, as firms which specialised in industry or banking moved into the other sphere, or as firms in the separate sectors amalgamated. Lenin seems to have derived this observation from the Austrian Marxist economist, Rudolf Hilferding's *Finance Capital*, which developed this[24] analysis principally through observation of the German economy. The third, and perhaps most crucial pillar of Lenin's thesis was the increasing propensity of monopoly capitalism to seek new outlets for investment overseas, as the declining profit rate in the advanced capitalist world forced the export of capital to virgin sources of cheaper raw materials, land and labour. For Lenin this was the principal driver of imperial expansion; the need to open new avenues for investment and to protect them. Lenin particularly acknowledged the validity of aspects of Hobson's underconsumptionist analysis, which he used as a key source in his writing on imperialism.[25] While Lenin made no direct reference to Luxemburg's theory, historians have suggested that he disagreed profoundly with her view that the spread of capitalism to the colonial world could extend the system's lifespan, and indeed he does imply in his writings that her emphasis upon the importance of empire as a market for commodities unsaleable in the domestic market, was rather the principal feature of an earlier stage of capitalist development.[26]

The fourth element in monopoly capitalism was the growing sophistication of the institutions of finance capital which made the seeking out of foreign opportunities and the channelling of investment overseas much easier to accomplish than before. On this point it is important to recognise that Lenin did not view imperialism solely as an intercontinental phenomenon, of Europe conquering Asia and Africa. The extension of the interests of monopoly capitalism within and across the states of Europe itself was a vital part of that process. For example, Lenin estimated that about half of German foreign investment stayed within Europe, as did about 60 per cent of French investment.[27] In fact for Lenin, imperialism had become not just a mere scramble for colonies in the less developed world, but a concerted effort by the forces of monopoly capitalism to carve up between themselves the whole of the world's resources and markets.

Here the fifth and final element of monopoly capitalism was essential in making this possible: the political dominance of the advanced capitalist nations by the small and fabulously wealthy bourgeois elites, and their ability to utilise and direct the coercive powers of the state to achieve their goals. As with Hobson, one is left with an image of politicians as the puppets of capitalist economic interests. Lenin believed that war and conflict was inevitable in this new era, because of the uneven development of capitalism among the nation-states. Britain, as the most advanced capitalist nation-state had already established hegemony over a substantial portion of the world's resources; but as other nations also underwent capitalist development, it became imperative to challenge the British for a bigger share of global assets. Since the British were not prepared to meekly surrender their advantages, violent confrontations were unavoidable. In this new era of impe-rialist conflict, Lenin saw the beginning of the final demise of capitalism. Ruinous wars would disrupt the international economy, intensify proletarian hardship and misery, whilst simultaneously arming them. The scene would be set for an international proletarian revolution, which would usher in the final epoch leading to communism.

The references in Lenin's work to Hobson, and the former's rather patronising agreement with many of the conclusions reached by the latter regardless of his suspect 'social-liberal' political beliefs, have contributed to a tendency to see the two theories of imperialism almost as a single, coherent thesis.[28] There are indeed many common elements: the emphasis upon domestic poverty and underconsumption as a factor driving investment overseas, and the paramountcy of capitalist financiers in shaping imperial policy to name but two. Certainly, these shared arguments have invited subsequent critics to direct the same attacks upon both of them, occasionally referring to their work as the 'Hobson-Lenin' thesis.[29] Historians such as Fieldhouse have stressed the importance of the similarities, in particular the centrality of metropolitan economic motives for expansion.[30] Others have challenged this imposed fusion. Eric Stokes and Norman Etherington both stressed the differences: Hobson's focus upon extra-European colonialism, compared with Lenin's particular interest in European imperialism, Lenin's specific concern with explaining the origins of the First World War in contrast with Hobson's main preoccupation with the evolution of British imperialism. Stokes in particular noted that while Hobson saw imperialism as beginning in about 1870, Lenin dated the commencement much later, at the turn of the century. A. M. Eckstein, in one of the most recent contributions to this debate, restates the case for treating the theories as a coherent entity.[31] Eckstein's comparison of the two theories concludes that while Lenin did not include the colonial expansion of the post 1870 period in his chronological categorisation of imperialism, his description of the driving forces behind it were so close to Hobson's view that the two can be deemed to be almost identical. Added to this, the extensive and acknowledged use of Hobson as a source by Lenin, clinches the validity of treating the two theories as the same.[32]

But it does seem that two crucial differences between the theses have been underestimated by Eckstein. First, the ideological gulf between the two men was fundamental, and the resolutions of imperialism they projected were starkly different. Hobson believed that while imperialism was a consequence of capitalist development, it was neither inevitable nor irreversible. For him, imperialism signified a dysfunctional capitalist system, a distortion of the 'true' historical development of capitalism, caused by the emergence of monopolies which exacerbated social inequality and underconsumption. He believed that the redistribution of wealth through progressive taxation and social reform could reverse this tendency by boosting the purchasing power of the poor and diminishing the problem of underconsumption. The recovery of the domestic market which followed would reduce the trend towards capital export, as investment in firms producing for the domestic market revived. It followed that the urgent need felt by financiers and investors to protect their overseas assets through imperial expansion would also diminish. Thus the driving force behind imperialism could be contained and reversed within the context of a reformed capitalism. Lenin, on the other hand, saw no alternative for capitalism other than the relentless pursuit through overseas imperialism of cheaper factors of production. The key problem for capitalism was the inevitable reduction of the profit rate, wrought by the spiralling costs of renewing the technologies of production. Significantly, Hobson's work did not include this concept of the alleged consequences of technological renewal for the profit rate, and it is this which accounts for the contrast in the optimistic prognoses of the two men: Hobson the Liberal's belief that capitalism could be saved and imperialism reversed, and Lenin the revolutionary's conviction that imperialism was unavoidable and would help to ensure the inevitable destruction of capitalism.

Secondly, there were quite sharp differences in the analyses of capitalism offered by Hobson and Lenin. Although Hobson did write about rival European empires, his main preoccupation was with the British, particularly those aspects of the metropolitan economy which drove expansion forward.[33] Hobson's description of British capitalism at the turn of the century differed profoundly from the generalised account of advanced capitalist development in Lenin's writing. Hobson described an economy sharply divided between an industrial 'producers' sector, located in the north and 'Celtic' fringe, and a financial or 'consumers' one, located in London and the south east. Hobson noted that the links between the two were few, and that the political and socio-logical consequences of this division were far reaching. In the north and the provinces, social relations were heavily coloured by the emergence of an industrial working class, much of which was organised, pugnacious and frequently inclined to challenge the authority of the bosses and the social elite. It tended to vote Liberal, though Labour emerged as a serious rival during Hobson's career. In the south east, where domestic employment and other service industries predominated, social relations were characterised by working-class deference to one's superiors and a tendency to vote Tory.[34] Of the two economic sectors, Hobson had little doubt that finance exercised the greater influence in defence of its interests. The huge profits generated by overseas investment, coupled with location in London, near the seat of political power, ensured that financiers, rather than industrialists, called the shots. The general picture of international capitalism in Lenin's work is profoundly different, of a merging of financial and industrial interests to create the monopoly capitalist 'finance capital' originally identified by Hilferding. Lenin was certainly aware of Hobson's work and aspects of it, notably the belief that industry was in decline and being undermined by financial inter-ests, was accepted by Lenin as the likely fate of some advanced capitalist nations. But the contrast between Lenin's 'fusion' and Hobson's 'fission' characterisation of the relations between indus-trial and financial capital remains.[35]

Efforts to locate the origins of imperialism in the field of metropolitan capitalist development met stiff contemporary resis-tance, particularly from Joseph Schumpeter (1883–1950).[36] Born in the Austro-Hungarian empire, Schumpeter was the grandson of a textile entrepreneur. In 1906 at the age of 23 he became one of the youngest men in Austria ever to win a doctorate, which was awarded to him by the University of Vienna. In the years before the First World War he pursued first a legal and then an interna-tional academic career as an economist in Austria, the Ukraine and the USA. Like his influential contemporary Rudolf Hilferding, Schumpeter was very much a product of the Austro-Hungarian empire, the troubled and decaying autocracy which dominated central Europe. Such was his status at the end of the First World War that in 1919 he served briefly as the Minister of Finance in the post-imperial Austrian regime. Schumpeter had long been a passionate advocate of free market capitalism, and he did not see it as the driving force behind the pre-1914 scramble for colonies. Instead, he looked to the ancient feudal political structures and culture of Europe to explain imperialism. This after all was the world he came to know well. He not only witnessed at first hand the cultural and political bellicosity of the Austrian and Russian empires, but also had the opportunity to compare them with the anti-imperial culture of the USA, where he worked briefly as a visiting professor in 1913. Significantly, Schumpeter wrote about imperialism just after the First World War, when the demise of the European empires of Russia, Germany and Austria seemed to offer a future in which imperial conflicts would be less of a threat.

Schumpeter's belief in free market capitalism led him to refute those like Hobson and Lenin who detected intrinsic patterns of development within capitalism which promoted imperialism. For Schumpeter, the essence of capitalism was those characteristics regarded by Hobson and Lenin as features only of its earliest stages of development; namely small firms, perfect competition, dynamic entrepreneurship and dispersed economic power and political influence. Schumpeter believed that these were the 'natural' systemic conditions towards which capitalism tended to evolve, if freed from the cultural and political constraints of pre-capitalist political and belief systems. The dynamism of capitalism arose from the activities of entrepreneurs, whose innovative efforts provided the springboard for leaps in productivity through the application of new technologies. It was they who were responsible for the impressive surges of economic growth which distinguished capitalism from earlier economic systems.[37] As capitalism spread across the world, so it promoted the trade, economic interdependence and global harmony celebrated by mid-Victorian Manchester liberals like Richard Cobden. Since capitalism thrived in conditions of international peace, stability, low taxation and minimum government, it followed that the 'natural' ideology of capitalism was profoundly anti- militaristic and anti-imperialist. The problem for

Schumpeter was the diversion of capitalism from this path in the late nineteenth century, as it embraced monopolistic practices, militarism and imperial conquest. According to Schumpeter, the reasons for this did not lie in the nature of capitalist development itself, but in the continuing survival of pre-capitalist political institutions and social value systems, which distorted capitalism's logical progress towards peaceful internationalism. While Schumpeter conceded that capitalism in many of the advanced nations at the beginning of the twentieth century demonstrated the monopolistic tendencies of concentrated ownership, restricted competition and protectionism, he saw this not as the working out of any internal dynamic of the system, but rather as the result of prevailing political systems and cultural climates which were inimical to the true nature of capitalism. The feudal monarchies and aristocracies which dominated Europe before 1914, with their fierce determination to keep mass democracy at bay, were committed to outmoded perceptions of the world which placed a premium on the aggressive acquisition of land, trade and other resources at the expense of rival kingdoms and nations. The political manifestations of this included imperialist expansion, protectionist tariffs and elitist economic and social policies designed to meet the interests of wealth and status at the expense of the masses. Schumpeter believed that this dominant culture of greed, aggression and anti-democratic elitism had perverted the course of capitalist development. By curbing competition, tariffs promoted the growth of powerful monopoly capitalist companies and cartels, while the prevailing culture of elitism, nationalist xenophobia and imperialist ambition seduced leading capitalists to the cause of conquest and international aggression, who were frequently tempted by such short-term imperatives as the need for new export markets and sources of raw materials. In this respect Schumpeter saw imperialism as atavistic, the consequence of attitudes, institutions and values which had outlived their time. The 'cure' was not reform of capitalism *per se*, but the democratisation of the advanced capitalist societies, and the sweeping away of feudal institutions and beliefs. Such change would allow truly pro-capitalist political institutions and cultural norms to dominate, ushering in a new world order of capitalist nations, imbued with the spirit of free competition, social mobility and international nonaggression and co-operation. Schumpeter believed that the USA, a nation born out of rejection of empire, epitomised the anti-imperialist nature of the truly capitalist society. It is therefore perhaps unsurprising that much of the latter part of his career was spent at Harvard. Writing shortly after the end of the First World War, and the dismantling of several major European empires and monarchies, Schumpeter must have viewed the post-Versailles world with optimism and hope. One can only speculate that his disillusionment at the rise of Fascist, Nazi and Communist totalitarianism in the inter-war period must have been as bitter as Lenin's realisation that the imperialist war of 1914–18 did not after all presage the demise of capitalism and worldwide workers revolution.

In spite of Schumpeter's rejection of Eurocentric economic theories of imperialism, the work of Hobson, Lenin and their adherents held a prominent position in the academic analysis of imperialism for almost half a century. Nonetheless, British academics were sceptical about the notion that the phenomenon could be explained solely by reference to national or sectional economic interests. The major British work in the field during the first half of the twentieth century was the *Cambridge History of the British Empire*, published in nine volumes between 1929 and 1959. It was a collaborative work edited by three established academics from Cambridge and London, E. A. Benians, J. Holland Rose and A. P. Newton. This vast work contained contributions from a large number of individual scholars, many from the empire itself. Written during a period when the ravages of the two world wars and the international depression of the 1930s made the decline of the British empire seem ever more likely, the work nonetheless conveyed a sense that the empire, for all its faults, had been a force for good in the world. There was a prevailing, but not uncritical, defence of the empire's record in safeguarding the welfare of subject peoples, and in establishing the economic and political basis for future progress towards national independence, prosperity and parliamentary democracy. This theme partly reflected a new emphasis in imperial policy on developing the empire, expressed in the Colonial Development Act of 1929 and the Colonial Development and Welfare Acts of 1940 and 1945. Most contributors eschewed any overarching economic interpretation of British imperialism, focusing instead upon analysis of developments in particular regions of the empire. It has been argued, however, that the *Cambridge History* laid the foundations for more detailed studies of the workings of empire at the periphery, and as such contributed significantly to later work which elevated the periphery over the metropole in explaining the growth and development of British imperialism.[38]

It was not until the 1950s and 1960s that a new and more incisive attack on Eurocentric economic interpretations of British and European imperialism was launched. This new wave radically challenged the definition of imperialism employed by Hobson, Lenin and earlier analysts of British imperialism, as well as their stress on the primacy of metropolitan developments in pushing empire forward. The two leading figures in this movement, John Gallagher and Ronald Robinson, sought to shift the location of the debate to the periphery of empire. In so doing, they came to establish a new orthodoxy explaining British imperial expansion; it forms the subject of the next chapter.[39] But the most direct rebuttal of Hobson and Lenin came from the adherents of the new school, who took Hobson and Lenin to task on their own terms. Prominent among them was D. K. Fieldhouse (b. 1925), whose 1961 article in the *Economic History Review* and 1973 work, *Economics and Empire 1830–1914*, challenged the view that the new colonies acquired by Britain in the late nineteenth century were major recipients of British overseas investment.[40] Born in India, Fieldhouse's career had close connections with empire. After teaching history at Haileybury public school, the former training institution for East India Company servants, in the early 1950s, Fieldhouse taught at the University of Canterbury in New Zealand between 1953 and 1957, and then became Beit Lecturer in the History of the Commonwealth at Oxford. An economic historian, Fieldhouse was profoundly influenced by the work of an earlier historian, Keith Hancock, who in the late 1930s had begun to survey the economic history of the empire. With the advice of Max Hartwell, a leading economic historian and his contemporary at Oxford in the late 1950s, Fieldhouse set about applying the latest statistical research on British economic history to British imperial development.[41]

Drawing upon work done in the 1950s by economic historians such as Cairncross and Nurkse on patterns of British overseas investment in the nineteenth and twentieth centuries, Fieldhouse argued that, in spite of the undoubted importance of overseas investment as a factor in the development of the British economy in the period, there was little correspondence between Britain's acquisition of territories in Africa and Asia, and the flow of investment to them either before or after British conquest.[42] In short there was little evidence that the tropical colonies which comprised much of the 'New Imperialist' acquisitions were significant for British investors or financiers. Systematically dealing with the various episodes of British imperial expansion during the period, Fieldhouse concluded that these incidents of expansion can be explained more convincingly by a host of other factors, usually connected with the collapse of local political order, rivalry with other expanding European empires, or pre-emptive annexations to avoid future strategic problems: difficulties arising at the periphery of empire rather than emanating from the metropole.[43] In addition to this critique, Hobson's notion that capital exports damaged the British economy by strengthening its competitors and 'starving' domestic industry of modernising investment has also been comprehensively dismissed. Cairncross and others point to the fact that investment in the developing world actually helped British industry by increasing the supply to it of cheaper raw materials and food. The British commitment to free trade therefore allowed capital exports to contribute to the competitiveness of British industry.[44] Furthermore, investment in the less developed world usually generated immediate demand for British manufactures. South American countries such as Argentina attracted large quantities of British capital to finance the construction of the country's railway system. Much of the capital equipment to build and run this had to be imported – from Britain.

New work on empire and overseas investment in the late 1980s provides stronger foundations for Fieldhouse's views on the absence of significant foreign investment in the colonies. Davis and Huttenback's *Mammon and the Pursuit of Empire* sustains a careful analysis of the direction of overseas investment, focussing not simply on the export of capital, but also taking into account investment in the British economy which was indirectly related to investment in the colonies.[45] They conclude that before 1900 only 20 per cent of all British foreign investment went into the empire, and only one third of that into the dependent empire, the implication being that there is little evidence to support Hobson's and Lenin's view that the new colonies were ever important conduits for profitable financial speculation.[46] But Davis and Huttenback do concede that even these small investments in the colonies may have been magnified in political importance by the fact that the British aristocratic and political elite were among their principal beneficiaries, since imperial investment seemed to attract this particular social class. As a consequence Davis and Huttenback postulate that government policy on empire might well have reflected this bias within the elite, given their dominance of Britain's political institutions.[47] Interestingly, this assessment of Hobson and Lenin does not entirely dismiss the notion of a powerful metropolitan vested interest group playing a role in the expansion of empire.

Indeed, the most recent attempt to construct an overarching explanation of British imperialism has sought to resurrect a metropolitan and economic dimension to the phenomenon. The full complexity of the 'gentlemanly capitalism thesis' of Cain and Hopkins will be explored in a later chapter, but here it is important to note that they, like Hobson, saw the investors of the south east, and the financiers of the City of London, as the principal promoters of British imperial expansion.[48] As such they have felt it important not only to acknowledge a certain intellectual debt of inspiration to Hobson, but also to defend certain aspects of his work in the face of some of the criticisms outlined above.[49] Cain's work on Hobson has been of particular importance. He robustly defends Hobson's analysis of a 'rentier' class of financiers and investors, located in the south east of England, led by an aristocratic elite who exercised a disproportionate degree of political influence in favour of imperial expansion.[50] Cain also points to recent research which suggests that Hobson's pessimistic estimation of the effects of foreign investment on the British economy, may have some merit. Perhaps most telling however, has been Cain's reiteration of Davis and Huttenback's challenge to the notion that the extremely modest amount of investment in the tropical colonies in the late nineteenth century disproves

Hobson's emphasis upon the primacy of foreign investment interests in the age of 'New Imperialism'. For Cain, Davis and Huttenback the issue is not the size or volume of such investment into the new tropical colonies, but their relative value to the politically influential interests who stood to gain or lose by them. In this respect the question was whether those whose money was at stake had the will and power to push government policy towards imperial conquest. Cain in particular believes that this was indeed sometimes the case.[51] Moreover, Cain points out that some of the countries and territories which Hobson saw as the victims of financially led British imperialism were in fact the recipients of very considerable capital exports; notably Egypt and South Africa.[52] He notes a tendency to overlook this by some of Hobson's critics.

But it is certainly not Cain's intention merely to resurrect Hobson. In a review of numerous episodes of colonial expansion, and the efficacy of the Hobsonian explanation of imperialism, Cain concludes that in every case, notably Egypt, South Africa and China, it is found wanting. Cain's sternest and most recurring criticism is of Hobson's tendency to see these episodes of imperial expansion as conspiracies, in which cunning and calculating financiers manipulated naïve or short-sighted politicians. For Cain and Hopkins, the mechanisms of 'gentlemanly capitalist' influence were subtle and negotiated, resting more on social kinship and 'like-mindedness' between the political and financial elites.[53] Theirs is, therefore, a partial rehabilitation of Hobson, and by implication of Lenin. But they have certainly revived metropolitan and economic explanations of empire and placed them once again at the centre of the historical debate.

Notes

1 E. E. Williams, *Made in Germany* (London, 1896); F. A. Mackenzie, *American Invaders* (London, 1902); A. Shadwell, *Industrial Efficiency: A Comparative Study of Industrial Life in England, Germany and America* (London, 1906).

2 K. Pearson, *National Life from the Standpoint of Science* (Cambridge, 1919); B. Kidd, *The Control of the Tropics* (New York, 1898).

3 S. Rowntree, *Poverty: A Study of Town Life* (London, 1901); C. Booth, *Life and Labour of the People in London* (London, 1892–97).

4 See S. B. Searle, *The Quest for National Efficiency: A Study in British Politics*

and Political Thought, 1899–1914 (Oxford, 1971).

5 For a particularly incisive study of the internal logic of tariff reform, see E. H. H. Green, *The Crisis of Conservatism: The Politics, Economics and Ideology of the Conservative Party 1880–1914* (London, 1995).

6 For example in A. Hodgart, *The Economics of European Imperialism* (London, 1977), pp. 24–30; W. J. Mommsen, *Theories of Imperialism* (London, 1980) pp. 11–19.

7 J. A. Hobson, *Imperialism: A Study* (London, 1902).

8 P. J. Cain, *Hobson and Imperialism: Radicalism, New Liberalism and Finance 1887–1938* (Oxford, 2002).

9 J. A. Hobson, *An Economic Interpretation of Investment* (London, 1911).

10 Cain, *Hobson and Imperialism*, pp. 233–40.

11 *Ibid.*, pp. 226–33.

12 Hobson, 'Free trade and foreign policy', *Contemporary Review* 74 (1898); 'Capitalism and imperialism in South Africa', *Contemporary Review* 77 (1900); 'The general election: a sociological interpretation', *Sociological Review* 3 (1910).

13 A. Smith, *The Wealth of Nations* (Harmondsworth, 1979).

14 P. J. Cain, 'J. A. Hobson, financial capitalism and imperialism in late Victorian and Edwardian England', *The Journal of Imperial and Commonwealth History* 13:3 (1985), 1–27.

15 *Ibid.*

16 K. Marx, 'The future of British rule in India', in K. Marx and F. Engels, *Selected Works* (Moscow, 1935).

17 K. Marx, *Capital*, 3 vols (Moscow, 1969).

18 D. McLellan, *Karl Marx: His Life and Thought* (London, 1983), p. 162.

19 R. Luxemburg, *The Accumulation of Capital* (London, 1951).

20 V. I. Lenin, *Imperialism: The Highest Stage of Capitalism* (Moscow, 1970).

21 For example, see the online version at www.resistancebooks.com.

22 See, for example, the introduction by Lewis and Malone in the Pluto Press reprint of 1996.

23 V. I. Lenin, *Imperialism and the Split in Socialism* (Moscow, 1972), p. 3.

24 R. Hilferding, *Das Finanzkapital* (Vienna, 1910).

25 Lenin, *Imperialism and the Split in Socialism*, p. 5.

26 W. J. Mommsen, *Theories of Imperialism* (London, 1981), p. 47; Lenin, *Imperialism and the Split in Socialism*, p. 4.

27 Lenin, *Imperialism: The Highest Stage of Capitalism*, p. 61.

28 Lenin, *Imperialism and the Split in Socialism*, p. 8.

29 A. M. Eckstein, 'Is there a "Hobson-Lenin thesis" on late 19th century colonial expansion?', *Economic History Review* 44: 2 (1991), 297–318.

30 D. K. Fieldhouse, 'Imperialism a historiographical revision', in K. E. Boulding and T. Mukherjee (eds), *Economic Imperialism* (Michigan, 1972), pp. 95–123.

31 Eckstein, 'Is there a "Hobson-Lenin thesis"?'.

32 *Ibid.*, pp. 310–13.

33 Hobson's views on the more general forces driving imperialism forward can be found in his article 'The economic taproot of imperialism', *Contemporary Review* 81 (1902).

34 Hobson, 'The general election: a sociological interpretation'; Hobson, 'The

two Englands', in J. A. Hobson, *The Modern Outlook* (London, 1910), pp. 302–10.

35 Cain, 'J. A. Hobson, financial capitalism and imperialism in late Victorian and Edwardian England', p. 10.

36 J. Schumpeter, 'The sociology of imperialism', first published in 1919, reprinted in his *Imperialism and Social Classes* (Oxford, 1951).

37 J. Schumpeter, *The Theory of Economic Development: An Inquiry into Profits, Capital, Credit, Interest and the Business Cycle* (New York, 1961), first published in 1911.

38 W. R. Louis, 'Introduction' of *The Oxford History of the British Empire Vol 5: Historiography* (Oxford, 1999), pp. 1–53; pp. 24–5.

39 J. Gallagher and R. Robinson, 'The imperialism of free trade" *Economic History Review* 6 (1953), 1–13.

40 D. K. Fieldhouse, *Economics and Empire 1830–1914* (London, 1973).

41 P. Burroughs, 'David Fieldhouse and the business of empire', *Journal of Imperial and Commonwealth History* 26:2 (1998), 6–27; 7–9.

42 Fieldhouse, 'Imperialism, a historiographical revision', p. 110. See also R. Nurkse, *Patterns of Trade and Development* (Stockholm, 1959).

43 *Ibid.*, p. 77.

44 A. K. Cairncross, *Home and Foreign Investment 1870–1915: Studies in Capital Accumulation* (Cambridge, 1953).

45 L. E. Davis and R. A. Huttenback, *Mammon and the Pursuit of Empire: The Economy of British Imperialism* (Cambridge, 1988), pp. 33–4.

46 *Ibid.*, pp. 37–8; p. 43.

47 *Ibid.*, pp. 278–9.

48 P. J. Cain and A. G. Hopkins, *British Imperialism 1688–2000* (London, 2001), pp. 34–8.

49 *Ibid.*, pp. 33–4.

50 P. J. Cain, *Hobson and Imperialism*, pp. 245–7.

51 *Ibid.*, p. 254.

52 *Ibid.*, pp. 254–5.

53 *Ibid.*, pp. 255–7.

4

Metropole, periphery and informal empire: the Gallagher and Robinson controversy of the 1950s and after

The Second World War wrought major changes in Britain's position in the world, severely weakening its economy, and confirming the USA as the new dominant global power. But British imperial pretensions died hard, and it was not until the early/mid-1950s that the longevity of the empire began to be brought into question. Nationalist resistance had already done for British rule in India and Burma in the late 1940s, while Arab nationalism first persuaded the British to leave Egypt, and then brought bitter humiliation upon them in the Suez crisis of 1956. The latter episode also underlined the fact that the new masters of the western world ruled from Washington. Communal violence and resistance to British rule drove the British out of even those colonies deemed to be of crucial economic importance, such as Malaya, while during the late 1950s black African nationalism presaged the end of empire there also. The decade ended with Macmillan's 'winds of change' speech in Africa, seen retrospectively as the death knell of the British empire as a premier international power.

Such was the context in which a radically new interpretation of British imperial history appeared: John Gallagher's and Ronald Robinson's thesis of 'free trade' imperialism.[1] In one short article in the *Economic History Review* they offered a completely new definition of imperialism, a new interpretation of the reasons for imperial conquest, and a new geography and chronology of the British empire. Just as the ideas of Hobson, Lenin, Schumpeter and others had been shaped by observations of their contemporary world, so also were those of these two Oxbridge academics.

Both men grew up in the twilight of empire. Robinson (1920–99) in particular was shaped by personal experience, serving with the RAF in Rhodesia during the war. War and its aftermath shaped the perspective of the two men. Both were non-Marxist socialists, worried by the post-war division of the world into western capitalist and eastern communist blocs. Their ideas on the British empire were influenced by this phase of transition in which British imperial power was being displaced by a new kind of American empire, which depended upon indirect economic and political control over client states, rather than direct colonial rule. These informal methods of imperial rule were increasingly employed in Asia and Africa in the 1950s, as American power grew. Gallagher and Robinson identified elements of continuity in British and American imperialism, particularly the exercise of influence as a technique of subjugation in preference to conquest. Informal persuasion instead of costly aggression rendered empire palatable to the liberal democratic politics which emerged in Britain during the nineteenth century, and which formed the domestic backdrop to American hegemony after 1945. Gallagher and Robinson's leftist politics tilted their sympathies towards the subjects of empire on the periphery, and contributed to their perception that conditions at the edge of empire were more important than developments in the metropole in both driving imperial domination forward and determining the form it took. Some historians argue that in *Africa and the Victorians* for example, their interpretation of the Egyptian uprising of 1882 which precipitated the British invasion was much influenced by the eerily similar events of 1956, when another Egyptian nationalist leader, Colonel Nasser, came close to suffering a fate similar to the nationalist leaders of the 1880s.[2] Their positions in British academia certainly helped consolidate their influence over the study of the British empire. John Gallagher (1919–80) was first Beit Professor of the British Commonwealth at Oxford, and then Vere Harmsworth Professor of Imperial and Naval History at Cambridge from 1971. In the same year, Robinson moved from Cambridge to take up Gallagher's former position of Beit professor. Together they exerted huge influence over imperial scholars from the 1950s to the 1980s.

At the heart of their thesis was a new understanding of imperialism. Gallagher and Robinson noted that previous writers had defined empire as territories conquered and directly governed by the British; the parts of the world 'coloured red on the map'. Imperialism thus implied 'formal' rule, the direct governance of territories acquired usually by armed intervention, and maintained by the imposition of direct rule by British officials and institutions, backed by force if necessary. Gallagher and Robinson argued that Britain's empire stretched much further than just the territories under such formal rule; that large swathes of the world were subject to indirect forms of British domination, which did not involve conquest or rule through imposed British personnel or official structures. This 'informal empire' was held together by a variety of means, some of which rested upon the actions or strategies of the British state, and others which relied upon unofficial channels of influence and power. The main pillar of informal imperialism was Britain's spectacular economic expansion after the industrial revolution. Gallagher and Robinson argued that the development of Britain's export trades in manufactures, capital and people were powerful forces which placed the country at the centre of the international economy. In most instances, the relations with other countries which emerged from this were peaceful and conducted more or less on a basis of equality. In a few cases, however, the relationships were far from equal. Some less developed countries and territories became economically dependent upon the Britain for capital investment, supplies of manufactures or as an export market. This dependency delivered political leverage into British hands, enabling various agencies of British imperial power, private or official, to compel local rulers to accommodate British requirements and demands. In the Victorian period, this frequently entailed the opening of the less developed country's market to British commerce. Such concessions were extracted from polities all over Asia and Africa, argue Gallagher and Robinson, but with particular success in Latin America. Countries which had recently emerged from Spanish or Portuguese colonial rule, such as Argentina, Mexico and Colombia, found themselves turning to the British for financial assistance, and in return opening their economies to British exports.[3] Over time, local elites in Latin America became dependent upon the British for financial support, supplies of manufactures, and as a market for the export of their primary produce – a relationship of 'informal imperialism' was thereby established. The British were able to extract policies congenial to their interests, particularly free trade, without having to resort to direct coercion. In this description, informal empire was an unintended by-product of British economic expansion, resulting more from local political instabilities and frailties at the periphery of empire, than any metropolitan drive for imperial conquest.

But Gallagher and Robinson also acknowledged that informal empire was not always an economic phenomenon. Sometimes force was used not to conquer but to intimidate or achieve limited control of key assets. For example, they cite the British seizure of the Cape early in the nineteenth century as a limited acquisition of territory designed to protect British access to the Indian Ocean. Inadvertently, it also delivered indirect control over much of southern Africa, particularly the areas of Boer settlement.[4] Such exercise of informal rule was frequently stimulated by the need to secure strategically vulnerable territories on the edge of formal empire. In the case of India for example, adjacent states such as Afghanistan or Burma were particular targets for British interference, because there was a perceived threat of incursion by rival European imperialism. British involvement in local political affairs might also be intensified if it was feared that local instability would lead to political collapse, and create a power vacuum into which rival European imperialists might be drawn. Again, however, it was circumstances at the periphery of empire, not developments in the metropole, which was the decisive factor in prompting formal imperial intervention.

Armed with this new conception of imperialism, Gallagher and Robinson were able to redefine both the geography and chronology of British imperialism. Whole regions of the globe, previously regarded as free of British rule, were now brought within the ambit of British imperial history. Latin America was the most startling example of this new trend. The absence of significant formal British colonialism on the continent had meant that before Gallagher and Robinson there was little historical interest in the British presence there. After Gallagher and Robinson, it became a major focus of study in informal imperialism. Perhaps even more significant was the new interpretation of the evolution of the British empire which the concept of informal imperialism made possible.

Previously, historians and other commentators had identified two distinct phases of British imperial expansion, driven by radically different ideologies, separated by an intervening period of anti-imperialism in which expansion all but ceased. The first phase was the great mercantilist era straddling the seventeenth to early nineteenth centuries, in which America was colonised and lost, only to be replaced by a new eastern empire in India. The victory of 'laissez-faire' liberal ideology in the heyday of the industrial revolution then ushered in a new scepticism towards empire. The costs involved in conquest and rule threatened to inflict cripplingly high levels of taxation on those classes whose enterprise had fashioned the British economic 'miracle'. Earlier mercantilist theories about economic growth, which stressed the importance of international trade, and the need to exclude rival European powers from trade with British colonies, gave way to the new ideas of Adam Smith and his adherents. These dictated that free trade rather than imperial possessions would deliver national prosperity and strength. Empire served only a small collection of interested groups at the expense of wider national interests. Among these were the chartered companies (such as the East India Company) who enjoyed privileged monopolies, and the military establishment which commanded a large proportion of the resources of the state. While imperialism inevitably brought war, free trade promised international interdependence and peace. The growth of this new anti-imperial ideology, particularly within the emerging Liberal Party, and its apparent victory in the mid-nineteenth century, convinced many contemporaries and later historians that mid-Victorian Britain was anti-imperial in sentiment. While this was never strong enough to inspire active decolonisation, it at least curbed the expansionism of the mercantilist era. But after 1870, 'anti-imperialism' gave way to 'New Imperialism', as the rival European powers, including Britain, carved up the continents of Africa and Asia between them. As shown, Hobson and Lenin believed that this new phase reflected metropolitan economic developments in the advanced capitalist world, and although others such as Schumpeter disagreed with this diagnosis, they nonetheless conceded that there was a new imperialist aggression abroad in the later nineteenth century which marked a break with the immediate past.

The concept of informal empire allowed Gallagher and Robinson to completely overturn this chronology of empire. They argued that the anti-imperialist ideology of the mid-Victorian political establishment cloaked a continuing policy of imperial expansion, the momentum of which had barely slowed since the late eighteenth century. Britain's spectacular economic growth fuelled an unprecedented surge of overseas economic expansion in the form of increased exports of manufactures and imports of food and raw materials to sustain British economic development. It had also unleashed a flood of British investment overseas. Most of this expansion was with stable and developed parts of the world, such as the USA, and posed no problem. But where British overseas interests flourished in regions of instability, it was necessary to protect them, regardless of the anti-imperialist rhetoric of politicians and ideologues in London and Manchester. Informal empire was the means by which this could be accomplished, without offending the pacific and fiscal sensitivities of the mid-Victorian establishment. While conquest and formal rule meant risk and expense, informal influence was relatively safe and cheap. Thus British informal imperial power expanded in the supposed era of 'anti-imperialism', spreading informal British hegemony in Latin America, Africa, and China.[5] The progress of this informal imperial expansion could be charted by the numerous treaties of free trade and friendship signed between Britain and the newly subordinated powers during the period.[6] Gallagher and Robinson also contended that anti-imperialism was never as strong as contemporaries and historians claimed. In spite of all protestations that empire was expensive, inhumane or immoral, mid-Victorian governments were prepared to use force if vital British interests were threatened. They noted, for example, that between 1841 and 1851, New Zealand, the Gold Coast, Labuan, Natal, the Punjab, Sind and Hong Kong were all absorbed into formal empire, while in the following twenty years, such territories as Lower Burma, the Transvaal, Lagos and Basutoland all became British possessions.[7] The mid-Victorian aversion to formal empire was thus largely cosmetic. Vital British global economic interests had to be defended, in Gallagher and Robinson's words, 'by informal means if possible, or by formal annexations when necessary'.[8]

Gallagher and Robinson conceded that the 'New Imperialism' of the post 1870 period represented a shift in the character of British imperial expansion, but they insisted it was not a resumption of expansion following a period of anti-imperial inactivity, as depicted by Hobson, Lenin and others. Instead, most incidents of imperial conquest represented a shift to formal rule in territories over which the British had previously exerted informal hegemony. The conquest of states in Africa, particularly Egypt in 1882, were examples of the British switching to formal control in response to concerns about the ineffectiveness of informal dominance.[9]. There were several reasons for this general transition to formal empire. The first was the emergence of a powerful European challenge to the British in the non-European world, arising from the modernisation of the economies of France and Germany, and latterly Tsarist Russia. Whereas in the mid-Victorian period the British, as the first and leading industrial nation, enjoyed a free run in the markets of the less developed world, European industrialisation and overseas economic expansion in the last quarter of the century presented the elites of Asia and Africa with alternative sources of economic sustenance and help. It therefore became easier for local rulers to flout British informal control, and to the alarm of British officials at the periphery, created the possibility of drift into the informal empires of Britain's European rivals.[10] A second source of difficulty was the impact of extended exposure of the more fragile pre-industrial economies to the full force of British economic expansion. Gallagher and Robinson believed that this could have the most destabilising consequences. Citing the example of Egypt, they contended that the governing structures of some less developed countries simply collapsed as trade and economic contact with the British gave rise to new social groups able to challenge ruling elites, or alienated other groups who were vital to maintaining the political status quo. These arguments were fleshed fully out in a brief chapter in the ninth volume of *The New Cambridge Modern History* published in 1962.[11] Faced with the threat to their interests posed by internal chaos, the British frequently could find no alternative to outright annexation. Thus, while post 1870 saw a change in the general form of British imperial expansion, it by no means represented a 'new' and separate phase of imperialism, merely the continuance of an existing trend by different means.

A central tenet of the Gallagher and Robinson thesis was that the decision to shift from informal to formal imperial rule was rarely precipitated by forces or developments in the metropole. Rather it was events at the periphery, such as the actions of rival European powers, or local political collapse, which triggered forward movement of the empire. Their later work stressed further the importance of the periphery as the source of imperial expansion. In *Africa and the Victorians: The Official Mind of Imperialism*, a study of British expansion on the continent, Gallagher and Robinson fleshed out their emphasis on the periphery as the taproot of British imperialism.[12] In particular they explored the mindset and assumptions of Victorian politicians and civil servants engaged in the formation of British imperial policy. They argued that there was an 'official mind' of imperialism, which was guided by certain key principles and attitudes.[13] These tended to predominate regardless of the party or individual politicians in power. In fact Gallagher and Robinson saw a striking similarity in the attitudes to empire struck by both Liberal and Tory politicians, irrespective of their conflicting rhetoric on empire. Senior government ministers and officials in such government departments as the Colonial and India Offices were drawn from the elite ranks of the aristocracy, and imbued with a lofty detachment which made them sceptical about businessmen and others from the lower ranks of society. Far from being the puppets of commercial men, Victorian politicians held their own views and priorities dear, and were intrinsically suspicious of those metropolitan business groups who lobbied for imperial conquest to defend their vested interests. Besides, the imperatives of laissez-faire political economy dictated that imperialist adventures of conquest were to be avoided if possible, since their expense threatened to undermine the principles of balanced budgets, low taxation and low government expenditure. This did not mean that overseas commercial interests were to go unprotected or ignored by the British state. Where ministers could use their influence and power to open overseas markets this would be done, provided that it did not involve excessive risk or financial cost. The exercise of 'informal imperialism' was acceptable, but the assertion of formal conquest was only a very last resort in cases where vital British interests were truly at stake. Generally, Victorian politicians insulated themselves against the demands and pleas of aggressive imperialist lobbies in Britain, frequently regarding them as selfishly rather than patriotically motivated, ignorant of conditions at the frontier of empire, and prone to exaggeration of the dangers there to British interests. Conversely, colonial officials and other British interests on the periphery could more effectively move London to action by virtue of their greater proximity and understanding of developments on the edge of empire. The importance of the 'men on the spot' was of course at its greatest before the construction of the imperial tele-graph network. The resolution of colonial crises, even if it meant imperial conquest, could not await directions from London which might take weeks or even months to arrive. The power to make crucial decisions had to reside in the hands of officials at the periphery, and London's role often only amounted to ratification or renunciation of actions long after the event. Even after the coming of the telegraph, there was still a heavy dependence on those with expertise in the field. The need for knowledge of local conditions, culture and the political situation always placed a premium on the views of imperial representatives on the periph-ery. Where such men advocated direct intervention or force, London was likely to comply. Gallagher and Robinson contended that in most instances of post 1870 British imposition of formal rule, it was British spokesmen on the periphery who persuaded government to sanction conquest, in some cases after the event.

Robinson later developed this focus on the periphery, by considering the means by which small expatriate groups of British officials or merchants within states subject to either formal or informal rule, could exert a disproportionate degree of political leverage to subordinate the local elite and the vast local popula-tion. Essential to the operation of empire were 'collaborators', significant groups within the local population who would act as advocates or instruments of British imperial power.[14] They frequently acted as intermediaries between the British and local rulers, ensuring that the latter accommodated the former wherever possible. Collaborators were drawn from a very wide range of groups; merchants, local chieftains, bureaucrats, revenue collectors – all could fulfil the role depending upon the requirements of the particular situation. Collaborators were also necessary where formal rule existed, limiting dependence upon expensive British manpower, and creating at least an illusion of local inclusion in imperial government. The Indian-born civil servant of the Raj and the powerless Malay Sultan, turned out in the full trappings of royal majesty on public occasions, were examples of collaboration at work. Successful co-option of local collaborators could preclude the dangers and expense of formal conquest. Loss of their allegiance could necessitate formal conquest, or in circumstances where direct British rule already existed, might cause rebellion and upheaval. The mutiny of the Indian sepoys in 1857 can be seen as a catastrophic breakdown of imperial collaboration. Once again, the heart of the argument is that the form and evolution of the empire was dictated by developments at the periphery rather than the metropole.

It is no exaggeration to say that Gallagher and Robinson revolutionised the debate about the British empire. So successful and persuasive was their approach that they became the effective leaders of a new 'school' of imperial history, which shared and developed their principles. In the early 1950s, even before Gallagher and Robinson, V. T. Harlow (1898–1961) argued that there was a 'long nineteenth century' of informal, free trade imperialism which seamlessly connected the empire of the late eighteenth century, with that of the later Victorian age.[15] There followed numerous general histories of the British empire and regional studies which seemed to support the concept of British intrusion into ostensibly independent countries early in the nineteenth century. The importance of events and developments at the periphery in prompting movements towards formal rule was stressed, and episodes of conquest were frequently presented as the concluding phases of longer periods of informal domination. In the early 1970s, D. K. Fieldhouse offered a general interpretation of British imperial expansion in the nineteenth century which drew heavily upon Gallagher and Robinson, emphasising the importance of peripheral factors in Asia as well as Africa.[16] Comprehensively dismissing the Hobson/Lenin metropolitan explanation of imperialism, Fieldhouse particularly stressed the role of European imperial rivalry in the late nineteenth century, and the strategic imperative to defend colonial borders, as recurring factors in imperial conquests. Other historians also sought to refine the analysis of developments at the periphery which stimulated the shift to formal empire. J. S. Galbraith identified the edge of empire as a 'turbulent frontier' where imperial control was tenuous or nonexistent, and where the uncontrolled agents of European expansion (merchants and missionaries) interacted with local societies.[17] All too frequently misunderstandings arose, as ambitious or zealous Europeans offended local laws and customs in their pursuit of profit or souls. Negative or racist perceptions of local cultures led to European insensitivity, while heavy-handed responses by uncomprehending local officials sometimes escalated minor squabbles into major confrontations with the local imperial power. Some historical case studies demonstrate how easily this could happen. O. B. Pollak showed that in Burma in 1851, it was the unrestrained activities of British merchants in Rangoon which triggered the second Anglo-Burmese war and the British annexation of Lower Burma.[18] British officials in India, unprepared to countenance defiance by neighbouring states lest this encourage rebellion within the Indian empire, reacted belligerently when some of the merchants were arrested for infringing local customs and laws. It was not just the colonial official at the periphery who could precipitate conquest; the untrammelled interaction of private British interests with the local authorities and society could also prompt aggression.

The explosion of regional case studies following the new emphasis on the periphery as the source of imperial conquest, offered new insights into how the destabilising consequences of commercial relations with the powerful British economy could push the British towards formal conquest. A classic example was Khoo Kay Kim's study of the western Malay states in the mid-nineteenth century.[19] Khoo Kay argued that the intrusion of British commerce into the western Malay states in the guise of Chinese tin mining, furnished rivals of the ruling Sultans with the resources to mount challenges to Royal authority. The civil wars which followed in the 1860s and 1870s ultimately compelled the British to assert more formal control over the western Malay states from 1874, in the form of 'advisory' British Residents at the courts of the Sultans. These Residents quickly came to exercise the real power of government in the Malay states. More recently, Thant Myint U notes that in Burma, it was the loss of the rice-producing territories of Lower Burma in the 1850s, together with the subsequent British direction of the rice trade of that region to meet the demands of the world market, which contributed to the food shortages, high inflation and social collapse which formed the backdrop to the final British annexation of what remained of the Burmese kingdom in 1885.[20] These are but two examples of a flourishing literature of case studies on destabilisation as a factor in British imperial conquest.

Of course, the Gallagher and Robinson thesis attracted critics as well as supporters. One of the earliest sceptics was D. C. M. Platt (1934–1989), who attacked the argument on several grounds.[21] An economic historian of Latin America first at Cambridge then at Oxford, Platt applied his specialist knowledge of British commerce at the periphery to test the Gallagher and Robinson thesis. He contended that in the early nineteenth century, the obstacles to the spread of British trade into the interior of some of the less developed regions of the world were far greater than Gallagher and Robinson allow. Poor transport and communications, hostility and resistance to foreign incursion into the local market, and sometimes the reluctance or inability of local populations living at subsistence level to buy British produce, all served to minimise the effects of British trade upon local society. This limited impact inevitably curbed the political leverage over local societies enjoyed by either the British government in London or British commercial interests at the periphery. Even with local collaborating interests working for the British, Platt is doubtful whether earlier in the century the British presence in many parts of Africa, Asia and Latin America ever amounted to more than a vague influence which was far more easily challenged or ignored than is suggested by the term 'informal empire'. Platt readily concedes that by the last quarter of the century British economic power was such that it did indeed pull many less developed countries into a subordinate relationship with the British, further reinforced by the expansion of British military power. But this merely strengthens Platt's central point that the 'New Imperialism' of the late nineteenth century was qualitatively different from Britain's presence in the less developed world in the mid-Victorian period, and not merely a continuation of imperial expansion by formal instead of informal means.

Another early critic was O. MacDonagh, who focused upon attitudes to empire in British domestic politics during the mid-Victorian period.[22] MacDonagh notes the intensity of much of the anti-imperialism among politicians between the 1840s and the 1860s as a factor to which Gallagher and Robinson pay far too little heed. For MacDonagh, the fierce antagonism felt especially by many Liberal politicians appears almost as 'closet imperialism' in Gallagher and Robinson's fleeting consideration of metropolitan party politics. As a result, they miss the fact that attitudes even among the Liberals became markedly more bullish towards empire towards the end of the century, not least in response to the perceived imperial ambitions of rival powers. MacDonagh is particularly critical of the way Gallagher and Robinson employ the term 'free trade' in the mid-nineteenth century context, pointing out that it was a coherent philosophy in British politics at the time which was steadfastly and overtly anti-imperialist. To infer that the ideology of free traders masked expansionist intent, is to misrepresent the motives and actions of its adherents. Again, the argument is that the differences in imperial policies between the mid- and later Victorian periods in imperial policy were ones of substance rather than mere form.

While the voices of MacDonagh and Platt were in the minority in the 1960s and 1970s, their criticisms have since resurfaced, albeit in amended form. The *Oxford History of the British Empire*, published at the end of the 1990s, contains several contributions in which the misgivings of Platt and MacDonagh are echoed. The celebrated historian of the empire, formerly of King's College London, Professor Peter Marshall (b. 1933), repeats Platt's doubts about the efficacy of British efforts to penetrate the less developed economies of Asia and Latin America in the early nineteenth century, and is even more sceptical about the extent of informal influence through political or diplomatic channels.[23] In the next volume, Martin Lynn reasserts Platt's contention that British trade was simply too limited to inflict a relationship of true dependence on most parts of the less developed world, at least before 1870.[24] He also reiterates the limited ability of British governments to assert authority over much of Africa, Asia and Latin America. While the British certainly came to enjoy great influence in many countries and territories, for Lynn the description of this as 'informal control' is both an exaggeration and a simplification of relations which were based on much more subtle and fluctuating processes of persuasion, in which coercion was rarely a clear final option.[25] Again by implication, Lynn's work suggests a qualitative shift in British relations with the less developed world in the last quarter of the nineteenth century, which marks 'New Imperialism' as a new and discrete phase of imperial development.

A more complex reassessment of Gallagher and Robinson has come from John Darwin, Beit Professor at Oxford and an eminent historian of British decolonisation. Much of Darwin's work tests the interpretation of British decolonisation as a conscious attempt by the British to lighten the load of imperial rule by replacing formal imperial rule by informal influence.[26] He therefore postulates Gallagher and Robinson's analysis of the later nineteenth century in reverse; a shift from formal to informal empire in order to reduce the burden of imperialism on a beleaguered metropolitan economy. The preoccupation with Gallagher and Robinson is no accident. In the preface to *Britain and Decolonisation* Darwin warmly acknowledged his debt to John Gallagher as a teacher and mentor. Recently Darwin has turned his attention to the more traditional arena of debate about the Gallagher and Robinson thesis, the late Victorian period.[27] For him, a puzzling aspect of the nineteenth-century British empire was its diversity of forms of rule, how this might be explained, and the extent to which it actually reflected consistency in the 'official mind of empire' in Whitehall.[28] Ultimately, Darwin is highly critical of the notion that there was ever a truly coherent official mind in London. He argues that numerous emerging factors made it increasingly difficult for politicians and civil servants to adhere to any established principles in the handling of imperial affairs. The political pressures from below in

Britain's emergent but volatile democracy, the unforeseen problems thrown up by the rapidity of social change in a fast industrialising society, and the rapid frequency of foreign and imperial developments, all combined to frustrate efforts to sustain a consistent policy in any area of government, let alone one as complex as imperial affairs.[29] In Darwin's words, 'ministers and officials were rarely free to impose their departmental view even when they had one'. In practice the opportunities for private commercial or other interests to exert influence over imperial policy were consequently far greater than Gallagher and Robinson believed. But Darwin agrees that those interests which were particularly well placed on the periphery were best equipped to secure concessions from the politicians. On this point Darwin offers the new concept of the 'bridgehead' to help explain the variations in the British imperial presence overseas.[30] The bridgehead was the collective presence of the British in a particular territory at the edge of empire. It usually consisted of an agglomeration of officials, merchants and missionaries, although the precise mix of occupations and talent always varied. Darwin argues that the precise nature of the British position, in particular whether it was able either to sustain effective informal influence or possessed the capacity to spur London to sanction conquest, was largely determined by the connexions and skills of this bridgehead. A bridgehead of commercial and other interests which enjoyed powerful and influential contacts in Britain, or with the ability to facilitate close relations with local collaborators, would be particularly well placed to impose an effective system of British informal rule, and if circumstances required, to persuade London to sanction formal rule. Thus for Darwin it was the character of the British enclave community at the periphery, its local and metropolitan political connexions as well as its talent and inclinations, which determined the nature of the British presence, imperialist or otherwise. This refinement of the Gallagher and Robinson emphasis on the importance of the periphery certainly invites new analysis of the various British ex-patriate communities around the world as a factor determining the nature of the British imperial presence.

Darwin's conclusions coincide with the slightly earlier work of the Vere Harmsworth Professor of Imperial and Naval History at Cambridge since 1992, C. A. Bayly (b. 1945) on the British conquest of India in the late eighteenth and nineteenth centuries. Bayly argues that it was the nature of the English East India Company's structure of authority in the east, its increasingly military character, and the high costs which that involved, which spurred on British expansion. As new Indian territories were acquired, heavy expenses were incurred in their governance and defence which could only be met by the acquisition of new lands from which taxes could be raised.[31] This process of cyclical conquest and financial crisis stimulating still further expansion, has been referred to as 'military fiscalism', a term which reflects the close relationship between military strength and the need to pay for it through tax revenues. Douglas Peers reinforces the importance of the militaristic character of the British presence in India as a factor which spurred on expansion.[32] While these interpretations do not especially cite Gallagher and Robinson as their inspiration, their detailed scrutiny of the Indian periphery, and the nature of the British presence there as a factor in the forward movement of empire, clearly owe much to the emphasis upon the imperial frontier which stems from Gallagher and Robinson.

In the mid-1990s a new attempt was made to reinterpret the rise of the British empire by P. J. Cain and A. G. Hopkins.[33] They are supportive of much of the Gallagher and Robinson thesis, particularly the concepts of informal empire, an 'official mind of empire' and the importance of factors at the periphery in stimulating imperial expansion. However, they contend that in rejecting metropolitan economic developments as a significant motor of imperialism, Gallagher and Robinson have restricted themselves to what is inevitably only a partial understanding of the phenomenon.[34] Cain and Hopkins argue that recent research demonstrates that there were in fact metropolitan-based economic developments and interests which drove expansion forward. These forces were mediated and shaped by conditions at the frontier of the empire in ways alluded to in the Gallagher and Robinson thesis, but to try to understand imperial expansion solely in terms of developments at the periphery is, in Cain and Hopkins' words, to mistake the symptoms for the cause. Cain and Hopkins certainly embrace key concepts like informal empire, but ultimately they judge the emphasis upon the periphery in the

Gallagher and Robinson school as excessive.

The Gallagher and Robinson interpretation is thus certainly open to question on a number of grounds. Firstly, the concept of informal empire is difficult to define clearly. How much influence over local political or economic elites is necessary to constitute a relationship of imperial domination? Historians are right to be uneasy about a concept of empire which was frequently not defined as such by contemporaries among both the imperialists and the imperialised, and which often went untested by events. When does the normal ebb and flow of power relations between nations become imperialist in nature? Uncertainty about whether a territory or state is subject to 'informal control' tends to undermine efforts to identify the chronological and geographical contours of empire. Secondly, it is certainly true that Gallagher and Robinson's work lacks any serious analysis or consideration of metropolitan economic or political developments. The revolution in British economic and social history since the 1970s has been fully utilised by Cain and Hopkins to expose this weakness even more clearly. The ideas of Gallagher and Robinson are engaging, but they can also be beguiling. One must look hard and carefully to satisfy oneself that these abstract notions actually apply to specific case studies of imperialism. Concepts such as informal empire and collaboration are unquestionably useful and appropriate tools for imperial historians, but they must be used with care. That said, there can be no doubt that these concepts and that of an 'official' mind guided by general principles of Victorian economy, represented a major leap forward for the study of imperial history when they were introduced in the 1950s and 1960s. They compelled historians to engage in more thorough and sophisticated analysis of relations between powerful and weak states, which incorporated the sociological and economic fields as well as the political. The focus on the periphery inspired a golden age of historical enquiry into many parts of the less developed world in Asia, Africa and Latin America which is still unfolding. In spite of misgivings, informal empire, collaboration, conditions on the periphery remain part of the stock in trade of the imperial historian, and there is little reason to believe that this will change in future. In this respect, the Gallagher and Robinson thesis continues to live and thrive.

The impact of the Gallagher and Robinson thesis on left wing perspectives of empire was quite profound. By the time of decolonisation in the 1950s and 1960s, in which communist and other left wing political movements played a leading role, many historians and theoreticians of the left had tended to assume that Marxist interpretations of imperialism had been vindicated by events. The new orthodoxy therefore came as something of a surprise. As a result, even though the peripheral school of thinking on British imperialism tended to eclipse earlier metropolitan economic explanations, there was something of a rearguard action from the Marxist left. From the 1950s onwards, Marxists sought to revise the Leninist interpretation of imperialism in the light of the early twentieth century proving not to be the 'highest stage of capitalism' predicted by Lenin. For them, the question of whether or not imperialism signifies that capitalism is in its death throes has been replaced by the issue of the gross international disparities of wealth and development which global capitalism has failed to remedy. Although much of this revisionist writing has focused upon imperialism in general, it has inevitably prompted some reassessment of the British empire's record on colonial economic development. The work of two Marxist writers, Paul Baran (1910–1964) and Andre Gunder Frank set the tone of this Marxist revisionism. Baran was a Russian-born, American-educated academic, whose main works on empire and economic development were published in the 1950s. He considered that factors which enabled capitalism to rapidly modernise the economies and societies of western Europe and other developed parts of the world.[35] Four developments were identified as crucial. Firstly, the modernisation of agriculture, which reduced the cost of food and, secondly, drove large numbers of peasants off the land to form a large pool of cheap labour for emergent capitalist industry to exploit at low wage levels. Thirdly, the division of labour created a class of merchants and entrepreneurs, who would be the main beneficiaries of the fourth and most crucial development, the accumulation of capital. The problem, argued Baran, was that those economies which developed capitalism earliest tended to be expansionist, seeking markets and sources of raw materials and other commodities in the less developed parts of the world. In so doing, they inevitably undermined the capacity of those less developed parts of the world to follow the path of advanced capitalist development. The main reason for this was that entrepreneurs from the more advanced capitalist economies quickly came to dominate the mercantile and agrarian sectors of the less developed economies, thereby undermining the emergence of local mercantile elites who, left to their own devices, would have accumulated capital and provided the leadership for modernisation of the local economy on capitalist lines. Even worse, these foreign capitalist 'cuckoos' tended to repatriate their profits, effectively stifling the local accumulation of capital which was so crucial for the process of capitalist modernisation. In addition, the swamping of local markets with cheap imports from the industrialised world undermined the local handicraft entrepreneurs who might have formed part of a local capitalist elite. In short, Baran argues that many parts of the less developed world found themselves in a 'no-man's land' of economic development, in which the worst features of the old feudal stage of development were entrenched, while the effect of western capitalist intrusion was to cut off the route to more advanced capitalist development.

Andre Gunder Frank's (b. 1929) career profoundly shaped his perspective on the impact of European colonialism on the less developed world. Born in Germany, this American educated Marxist enjoyed lengthy spells during the 1960s and 1970s at universities in Brazil, Mexico and Chile. In the latter, he was even an adviser to the left wing government of Salvador Allende, which was bloodily toppled in the military coup of 1973. This direct personal experience of the former European colonies of Latin America influenced Frank's work on the economic legacy of colonialism. He amended Baran's analysis by arguing that from the fifteenth century, as western European nations conquered large portions of Africa, Asia and South America, they created an integrated global capitalist system in which the economies of the less developed world were shaped and subordinated to promote their own rapid capitalist development.[36] This involved the domination of the productive assets of the colonies by the capitalist elites of the imperialist powers, and the progressive depletion of local capital surpluses to fuel the economic development of the imperialist nations. In addition, patterns of production, land ownership, transport and communications emerged which privileged the needs and demands of the imperialist economy over those of the colony. So entwined with the structures and priorities of their western capitalist masters, these colonial economies were prevented from developing along the same lines as the more advanced capitalist nations. Thus the international capitalist system served to accelerate the development of privileged and dominant parts of the world, whilst it progressively 'underdeveloped' subordinate colonies in Latin America, Asia and Africa. Frank's work focused principally upon Latin America, but he contended that his thesis, sometimes referred to as 'the development of underdevelopment' held good for other colonised portions of the world.

Frank's thesis gathered considerable support within the 'New Left' of the 1960s and 1970s, partly because of contemporary political trends in which 'Third World' poverty seemed not only the consequence of economic exploitation by western transnational corporations and the Cold War policies of American administrations, but also promised the most fertile ground for the advance of Marxist political movements. Other Marxists have sought to build upon Frank's framework, notably Wallerstein (b. 1930), whose two-volume analysis of the development of European global economic hegemony between 1500 and 1750, was solidly based on Frank's concept of an emergent global economic system which exploited the non-European world for the benefit of Europe's emergent capitalist nations.[37] Like Baran and Frank, Wallerstein was a product of American academia. However, even within the Marxist camp there have been sceptics; for Bill Warren, a British communist who died in the early 1990s, Frank's departure from classical Marxist theory, in which capitalism transformed the world, spreading its 'core' features of industrialisation and class conflict, was a step too far. Warren contended that contrary to Frank's thesis, some parts of the postcolonial world were in fact in the process of embarking upon the rapid capitalist modernisation deemed impossible in Frank's model.[38] Though this view was greeted with scepticism by other Marxists at the time, the startling economic progress made by some of the East Asian 'tiger' economies in the 1980s and 1990s has tended to support Warren's argument, whilst calling the underdevelopment thesis into question.

The tendency of Marxists to treat imperialism as a global and international phenomenon has tended to preclude specific examination of the British empire, though their analyses inevitably include a substantial comment on British imperialism. Certainly the question of the effects of British imperialism on the long-term economic fortunes of the colonies both before and after independence has figured prominently in historical writing on the British empire, and as such has provided something of a testing ground for some of the arguments outlined above. As has been so often the case, studies of India have provided some of the most illuminating contributions. In fact, some of the earliest work of Indian historians on the economic consequences of British rule pre-empted the underdevelopment thesis. As early as 1871, D. Naoroji (1825–1917), the Indian nationalist leader and later British M.P., argued that the British authorities effected a 'drain' of Indian wealth to meet the servicing of debts to British investors, a view which was elaborated by the famous Indian economic historian R. C. Dutt (1848–1909) thirty years later into the thesis that trade and other policies enacted by the British, were designed to shape the Indian economy to meet British economic needs.[39] Dutt began his career as a civil servant in India, but developed a formidable reputation by the end of the nineteenth century as an Indian nationalist writer and activist. As Charlesworth points out, these were positions motivated largely by a desire to secure political reform, rather than purely academic analysis, and they were certainly not set within the more abstract Marxist framework of the dependency school.[40] But the issue identified was fundamentally the same, namely the effects of long-term economic interaction with the imperial metropole upon a colony's economic development. The long-running debate which has ensued about the economic consequences of British rule in India has indirectly influenced academic assessments of the dependency thesis.

The notion that the British drained India of capital and thereby stymied the prospects of an industrial revolution there has remained a compelling argument for some historians, particularly those of the Indian nationalist movement or the political left. Some recent historians have lent weight to the view that British conquest in the first half of the century did undermine indigenous channels of commerce and economic development, particularly with the disbandment of the private armies of formerly independent Indian states, which had constituted a significant consumer market for domestic produce.[41] Taking into account the surge of British investment into India in the later nineteenth century, particularly in the railways and other parts of the infrastructure however, the balance of historical opinion doubts that the scale of the drain was ever significantly large to tip the balance against rapid economic development.[42] In fact, it has rather leant towards the view that British imperial rule was ineffective in imposing consistent or decisive economic policies on India. For example, R. E. Frykenberg, Professor of History and South Asian Studies at the University of Wisconsin, shows that in south India at least, land taxation policies were frequently determined more by local conditions than efficiently administered British avarice.[43] Criticisms of British Indian development policy now tend to focus on sins of omission rather than commission; that the impact of modernising imperial forces such as foreign investment in the late nineteenth century was insufficient to accelerate growth above and beyond indigenous constraints.[44] In the case of India at least, the weight of scholarship is deeply sceptical about the thesis of underdevelopment.

More general analysis of the economic development of the British empire also tends to dispute New Left claims of imperialist indifference to questions of imperial development and the welfare of colonial peoples. Havinden and Meredith, respectively Senior Lecturers in Economic History at the Universities of Exeter in Britain, and New South Wales in Australia, show that in spite of the undercurrents of self interest and latent racism which underpinned British thinking about their colonial subjects, there was an emergent sense of obligation towards colonial economic development.[45] The origins of this lay in such Victorian notions as protecting traditional societies from the disruptive effects of imperial economic incursion (Trusteeship), and were elaborated in Joseph Chamberlain's ideas for fostering imperial unity, and promoting colonial economic development which would allow colonies to complement the productive capabilities of the metropole and other parts of the empire.[46] While parsimonious restrictions on state expenditure restricted late Victorian and

Edwardian governments to 'market-led' solutions for colonial problems of underinvestment which were of only limited effectiveness, Chamberlain was prepared to force legislation on the issue (Colonial Loans Act 1899; Colonial Stocks Act 1900).[47] This, and the extensive battery of twentieth-century legal reforms to promote development, indicates that there was at least a strand of imperial economic thinking which was sympathetic to the cause of colonial economic development, even if it secured only very limited advances.

In these ways research into the question of British colonial development has informed and influenced the debate about some of the New Left theories. It is fair to say that it has exposed the limited historical research undertaken to support the underdevelopment thesis by some of its key adherents. Moreover, in the British case, the flexibility in forms of rule and imperial economic strategies, which varied geographically and chronologically, make historians justifiably doubtful of theories which postulate coherent systems of imperial exploitation and underdevelopment. While Gallagher and Robinson and others are willing to concede the presence of an 'official mind of empire', it was never sufficiently intelligent or organised to weld the disparate parts into a planned or effective machine of expropriation. In this respect, the richness of historical empirical research on the British empire has largely rebutted these neo-Marxist theoretical models. As will be seen in the next chapter however, from the 1970s the empire became the arena for a new theoretical assault on history which challenged the very traditions of empiricism on which the subject has been traditionally based.

Notes

1 J. Gallagher and R. Robinson, 'The imperialism of free trade', *Economic History Review* 6 (1953), 1–15.
2 W. R. Louis, 'Introduction', in R. W. Winks (ed.), *The Oxford History of the British Empire Volume V: Historiography* (Oxford, 1999), pp. 40–1.
3 Gallagher and Robinson, 'The imperialism of free trade', 9–10.
4 *Ibid.*, 2
5 *Ibid.*
6 *Ibid.*
7 *Ibid.*, 2–3.
8 *Ibid.*, 3.

9 *Ibid.*, 13–14.

10 *Ibid.*, 13.

11 R. Robinson and J. Gallagher, 'The Partition of Africa', reprinted in W. R. Louis (ed.), *The Gallagher and Robinson Controversy* (New York, 1976), pp. 73–127.

12 R. Robinson and J. Gallagher, *Africa and the Victorians: The Official Mind of Imperialism* (London, 1965).

13 *Ibid.*, p. 20.

14 R. Robinson, 'Non European foundations of European imperialism: a sketch for a theory of collaboration', in R. Owen and R. Sutcliffe (eds), *Studies in the Theory of Imperialism* (London, 1972).

15 V. T. Harlow, *The Founding of the Second British Empire* (2 vols, London, 1952 and 1964).

16 D. K. Fieldhouse, *Economics and Empire 1830–1914* (New York, 1973).

17 J. S. Galbraith, 'The turbulent frontier as a factor in British expansion', *Comparative Studies in History and Society* 2 (1960), 150–68.

18 O. B. Pollak, *Empires in Collision: Anglo-Burmese Relations in the Mid-Nineteenth Century* (Greenwood, 1979), p. 80–2.

19 Khoo Kay Kim, *The Western Malay States 1850–1873: The Effects of Commercial Development on Malay Politics* (Kuala Lumpur, 1972).

20 Thant Myint U, *The Making of Modern Burma* (Cambridge, 2001), pp. 135–45

21 D. C. M. Platt, 'The imperialism of free trade: some reservations', *Economic History Review* 21 (1968), 298–306; 'Further objections to an imperialism of free trade' *Economic History Review* 26 (1973), 153–60.

22 O. MacDonagh, 'The anti-imperialism of free trade', *Economic History Review* 14 (1962), 489–501.

23 P. J. Marshall (ed.), *The Oxford History of the British Empire Vol. 2: The Eighteenth Century* (Oxford, 1998), pp. 23–5.

24 M. Lynn, 'British policy, trade and informal empire in the mid-nineteenth century', in *The Oxford History of the British Empire Vol 3*, pp. 101–21; p. 115.

25 *Ibid.*, pp. 119–20.

26 J. Darwin, *Britain and Decolonisation: The Retreat from Empire in the Post-War World* (Basingstoke, 1988), pp. 22–4.

27 J. Darwin, 'Imperialism and the Victorians: the dynamics of territorial expansion', *English Historical Review* (June 1997), 614–42.

28 *Ibid.*, 614–15.

29 *Ibid.*, 624

30 *Ibid,*, 629.

31 C. A. Bayly, *Imperial Meridian: The British Empire and the World 1780–1830* (London, 1989), pp. 59–60.

32 D. Peers, *Between Mars and Mammon: Colonial Armies and the Garrison State in India 1819–35* (London, 1995).

33 P. J. Cain and A. G. Hopkins, *British Imperialism* (Edinburgh, 2001).

34 *Ibid.*, pp. 26–30.

35 P. Baran, *The Political Economy of Growth* (London, 1957); see also C. A. Barone, *Marxist Thought on Imperialism: Survey and Critique* (Basingstoke, 1985), pp. 86–92.

36 A. Gunder Frank, *Capitalism and Underdevelopment in Latin America* (Harmondsworth, 1971).

37 I. Wallerstein, *The Modern World System: Capitalist Agriculture and the Origins of the European World Economy in the 16th Century* (New York, 1974); and *The Modern World System II: Mercantilism and the Consolidation of the European World Economy 1600–1750* (New York, 1980).

38 B. Warren, *Imperialism: Pioneer of Capitalism* (London, 1980).

39 D. Naoroji, *Poverty and UnBritish Rule in India* (London, 1901); R. C. Dutt, *The Economic History of India in the Victorian Age from the Accession of Queen Victoria in 1837 to the Commencement of the Twentieth Century* (London, 1902); N. Charlesworth, *British Rule and the Indian Economy 1800–1914* (London, 1982), pp. 11–12.

40 Charlesworth, *British Rule* p. 13.

41 C. A. Bayly, *Rulers, Townsmen and Bazaars: Northern Indian Society in the Age of British Expansion 1770–1870* (Cambridge, 1988), pp. 268–70.

42 R. J. Moore, 'Imperial India 1858–1914', in A. Porter (ed.), *The Oxford History of the British Empire Vol. 3: The Nineteenth Century*, pp. 422–46; see pp. 444–5; Charlesworth, *British Rule*, p. 69.

43 For example, see R. E. Frykenberg, *Guntur District, 1766–1848: A History of Local Influence and Central Authority in South India* (Oxford, 1965).

44 Charlesworth, *British Rule*, p. 69; Moore, 'Imperial India', p. 444.

45 M. Havinden and D. Meredith, *Colonialism and Development: Britain and its Tropical Colonies 1850–1960* (London, 1993).

46 *Ibid.*, pp. 1–24.

47 *Ibid.*, p. 89.

5

Cultural explanations of British imperialism I: post-colonial theory and its critics

In the 1970s European imperialism attracted the interest of intellectuals from outside the network of historians and social scientists who had dominated the field since the early twentieth century. From the 1950s the emerging school of thought which came to be known as cultural theory had undergone a revolution in thinking about culture and its role in the evolution of modern societies. In particular, scholars in the fields of linguistics, anthropology, philosophy and literature explored the role of culture (art, literature and more popular forms of culture such a film, TV and even advertising) as a language for the transmission of dominant ideas and values. It was argued that different cultural media contained their own complex structures of symbolism, which facilitated the indirect communication of values through inference and nuance, as well as the overt message contained within the film, book or other cultural medium. Structuralists, and later 'post-structuralist' thinkers argued that cultural artefacts ('texts' or 'discourses') could be analysed to bring forth the latent commentaries of attitudes and values contained within.[1] However, post-structuralists such as Jacques Derrida contended that the structure of hidden meanings and symbols was infinitely complex, with supplementary meanings and symbols arising from within every deconstructed hidden meaning, like the continuous dismantling of a Russian doll.[2] Ultimately Derrida and his followers believed that since all texts contained within them infinite complexities of interpretation, none could ever provide a truly accurate reflection of reality; all knowledge was imperfect, subjective and relative. The great project of the Enlightenment, the revealing of universal truths by the application of reason, was therefore an illusion. The best that could be done was to decode the values and beliefs which lay behind discourses through the systematic analysis of texts, whilst always conceding that objective truth about events and reality was beyond recovery.

The limits to knowledge implied in such an approach are inevitably controversial, and many historians, who believe that it is at least possible to establish certain indisputable facts about the past even if totally accurate reconstruction is impossible, are deeply sceptical. Even more challenging was Foucault's assertion that the interpretations of the past offered by history, like all discourses, are themselves instruments of political power, enabling those who dominate society to sustain their hegemony by controlling the parameters of what is accepted as reliable knowledge, and therefore eligible for inclusion in the agenda of intellectual and political debate.[3] History and all accepted academic knowledge therefore requires, like all discourses, systematic textual analysis in order to reveal latent assumptions, values and ideas which underpin the political hegemony they support.

It was perhaps only a matter of time before such ideas about the ephemeral quality of knowledge, and the need to deconstruct it in order to reveal underlying agendas of dominance, were turned to the phenomenon of imperialism. The interaction between different cultures, their perceptions of each other, and the assertion of power by one over the other, were all aspects of imperialist relationships which were intrinsically interesting for those engaged in cultural studies. Moreover, the persistence of racism in the west and quasi-imperialist aggression in the 'Third World', in spite of the supposed demise of colonialism in the great wave of national independence movements in the 1950s and 1960s, were phenomena which required explanation. Interestingly, the first foray into the arena of culture and imperialism came not from the postmodernists, but from the traditional Marxist left. Victor Kiernan (b. 1913), now Emeritus Professor of Modern History at the University of Edinburgh, was a leading figure in the school of British Marxist historians which emerged after the Second World War, whose ranks included such luminaries as Eric Hobsbawm, Christopher Hill, Rodney Hilton and E. P. Thompson. A product of Cambridge University in the 1930s,

Kiernan became an active member of the Communist Party in 1934, remaining an active member until 1959, when he followed other historians out of the Party in protest against the Soviet invasion of Hungary. He has however remained true to his Marxist beliefs. Kiernan saw the British empire at first hand, as a lecturer in India in the 1930s, an experience which infused his writing on imperialism with passion and confidence. Kiernan's work has covered a wide range of aspects of European and American imperialism in the nineteenth and twentieth centuries.[4] But perhaps his most celebrated work was *The Lords of Human Kind*, first published in 1969.[5]

Using the private papers, memoirs and literature of the European colonial elites, Kiernan traced the development of European colonial attitudes over several centuries. The Dutch, Spanish and other continental empires were considered as well as the British. Kiernan reached several conclusions, which have shaped the perceptions of numerous later historians. Firstly, he detected a deterioration of the value of the subject peoples in the eyes of the Europeans, especially during the nineteenth century. Earlier notions that indigenous peoples were capable of benefiting from the Enlightenment offered by European rule were displaced by a conviction of their inherent racial inferiority.[6] Secondly, from this developed a conviction that all cultural beliefs, values, religions and institutions of the subject civilisations were inconsequential, and based on superstition and primitive ideas.[7] Thirdly, by the end of the nineteenth century, Europeans had come to believe in a kind of taxonomy of the races, with the whites firmly at the apex of a hierarchy which categorised races in terms of their colour, on the principle that the darker the skin, the more primitive the people. Most valued where the so-called 'martial races' such as the Sikhs and Gurkhas of British India and Nepal, whose warlike 'virtues' rendered them useful to the imperial project. Even here, it was assumed that these natural warriors tended to be of lighter skin tone.[8] Fourthly, Kiernan argued that the emergence of this racist perspective of white cultural superiority sustained the contradiction of a trend towards popular democracy in metropolitan European societies such as Britain and France, just as their overseas empires were becoming even more despotic. Yellow, brown and black people were simply racially unfit for self rule or democracy. Herein lay the roots of later racist beliefs which survived the demise of the European empires which nurtured them.

Left wing intellectuals were deeply influenced by Kiernan's book, particularly Edward Said.[9] He was to draw from Kiernan's ideas and combine them with some of the new philosophical ideas of postmodernism. In 1978 Said's *Orientalism* was to prove a milestone in thinking about European imperialism.[10] Together with his *Culture and Imperialism*, published fifteen years later, *Orientalism* constituted a radical departure from previous approaches to the subject.[11] They are of particular significance for British imperial history, because Said (1935–2003) drew extensively from English literature to explore British attitudes to their empire. Said's personal background lent an unusual perspective to his work. Born to a wealthy Palestinian family in Jerusalem, Said emigrated to the USA at an early age, and received a western education. He claimed that the contrasting experience of being Arab, yet also the recipient of western culture and education, provided him with unique insights into the perspectives of both the west and the middle east. Politically to the left, and an ardent supporter of the Palestinian cause, Said became a controversial figure in American academe, occupying a prestigious Chair at Columbia University and achieving a high profile in the western media, whilst provoking often vitriolic attacks upon him by the pro-Israeli right in the USA. *Orientalism* secured for Said a prominent position not only in international scholarly circles, but also as a commentator on world events. Moreover, his work effectively gave birth to a whole new approach to the study of imperialism, referred to generally as either 'colonial discourse analysis' or 'post-colonial theory'. It rapidly rose to become a significant academic presence on both sides of the Atlantic. The reasons for this are not entirely clear, but one historian attributes the success of post-colonial theory to the discrediting of the Marxist materialist and class-based interpretation of history, following the defeat and fall of communism at the end of the 1980s. This forced many on the left to seek new explanations for historically uneven international distributions of power.[12] Cultural studies had also proved its ability to attract considerable media attention and academic cachet. As one commentator has rather cynically observed, Said's work made post-colonial literature 'one of the booming fields in English departments', while its leading exponents 'became superstars of the academic firmament'.[13]

The crux of Said's argument is that the stereotypical and racist perceptions of the conquered peoples of the European empires are of distant origin, and predate the modern age of European imperial expansion. In *Orientalism* the roots of the negative stereotyping of Muslims and the people of the middle east are traced back to the early middle ages, when Islam and European Christendom initially came into contact through trade, but more traumatically in a series of ideologically driven wars in Spain, the Holy Land, and later in the Balkans. In these conflicts, the European Christians rightly learned to fear their militarily superior neighbour, whose power took them to the gates of Vienna in the seventeenth century.[14] Little wonder that in medieval Christian ideology Islam and its middle eastern followers acquired an almost demonic quality, seeming to threaten the very survival of Christianity. Muslims were depicted in Christian writings as tyrannical, cruel, lustful, effete and treacherous – the living embodiment of diabolical human vices. Out of this emerged a more general and enduring perception of the orient as a place of decadence, corruption and menace. Said argued that western Christian culture's construction of this dystopian view of the east was not merely a terrified response to a formidable enemy. The orient was described as the opposite of the west, the antithesis of Christian civilisation. In defining Islam and the orient as a malign, malodorous, effeminate and alien 'other', Christian intellectuals were casting the Christian west as its opposite – benign, masculine, civilised, moral and virtuous. *Orientalism* traces the development of this self-validating portrayal of Islam and the east through the centuries into the modern age, arguing that herein lay a powerful motivational force behind imperial conquest. Thus the judgement of the twentieth-century Prime Minister Arthur Balfour, that for all their ancient history of great civilisations, the Egyptians were unfit to govern themselves, sprang out of centuries of European culture.[15]

Said contended that this cultural heritage of stereotyping the orient as inferior, in spite of its legacy of ancient 'civilisation', created a European mindset which made imperial conquest of such peoples less morally problematic, and for some easily defensible. Imperialism could be justified as extending the benefits of superior western civilisation to oriental peoples unfit to find it for themselves. In *Culture and Imperialism* Said asserted that the eighteenth and nineteenth centuries saw an intensification of this process of elevating Christian Europe through the creation of a negative non-European 'other'. Black Africans, yellow Chinese and indigenous peoples everywhere came to be depicted as barbarous, childlike, uncivilised and generally unfit to conduct their own affairs. The rise of nationalism was a particularly potent force behind this trend, extending negative cultural images of foreign 'others' to rival European powers as well as intensifying those of non-European subject peoples.[16] However, at the bottom of all western hierarchies of 'otherness' and inferiority were the subject colonial peoples who differed in colour, religious persuasion or both. These negative cultural stereotypes survived the demise of the great European formal empires in the decades following the Second World War, and continued to condition western political responses to the post-colonial world. Thus the violent interventions by the Americans and others in Korea, Vietnam, Chile, Nicaragua, Iraq and Afghanistan, were spurred on by surviving western cultural images of the inferiority and unfitness for self government of the peoples of these former colonies. Hence the title 'post-colonial theory' as an umbrella term for this branch of cultural studies.

Said's work captured the imagination of a new generation of scholars in the 1980s, especially in the former colonies, and gave issue in the following decades to a flourishing literature which developed the arguments of *Orientalism*. Post-colonial theorists in parts of the former British empire (especially India) became engrossed in the impact of western cultural stereotyping on the colonial peoples, particularly discourses about race. They sought to uncover the perspectives of imperialism of those on the receiving end of imperial dominance, whose powerlessness or illiteracy rendered them silent in the official accounts penned by the conquerors and their allies. Particularly significant was the emergence of 'subaltern studies', which sought to write the history of those who were the immediate subordinates of European rulers, by textually analysing the official records, distilling the perspective of the oppressed by imaginative deduction.[17] Such a complex approach was necessary because of the dearth of sources written by the subordinate (subaltern) peoples themselves; where such sources did exist, they were seen as being extremely important. However like other adherents of post-colonial theory, the subaltern studies group came to doubt the very foundations of historical analysis itself, since all such knowledge tends to be the product of western thought, assumptions and ultimately, power.[18] Instead, some advocated the construction of an alternative version of the past of the colonial subalterns, which did not rely upon historical evidence in western academia's sense of that term, and which gave prominence to myth and other indigenous versions of the past.[19] Some histories of gender and class in the empire have also drawn heavily upon post-colonial theory, notably Midgely's analysis of how the conquered lands and their populations were 'feminised' in western cultural representations to signify their inferiority, and Chakrabarty's study of the Bengali working class in the late nineteenth and early twentieth centuries.[20] As with other post-colonial theorists, these writers were rejecting the very foundations of historical study.

Perhaps inevitably, the 1990s saw a ferocious backlash from orthodox imperial historians. The departure not only from the commonly accepted principles of historical analysis, but from the basic precepts of western thought was simply untenable in the eyes of critics. John Mackenzie emerged as perhaps the most forthright, attacking post-colonial theory on a number of counts.[21] Based at the University of Lancaster, where he became Professor of Imperial History and a Fellow of the Royal Historical Society, Mackenzie emerged in the 1980s as the leading British historian of imperial culture. As editor of the influential Manchester University Press series *Studies in Imperialism*, he was instrumental in promoting the emergence of a cultural perspective in British imperial history. As will be seen in the next chapter, however, his approach contrasted sharply with Said's. The rejection of historical method in much post-colonial theory is a particular target for Mackenzie's ire, but the whole tenor of the approach is roundly condemned. He accuses post-colonial theorists of imposing their own, politically correct moral agenda upon their readings of the past, a tendency which he believes leads to oversimplification and a weak grasp of the historical context within which orientalist perspectives emerged.[22] Moreover, he contends that few post-colonial theorists have grasped the huge variety of western responses to the orient, or their transient character. For Mackenzie, western cultural perceptions of the east were not a monolithic monologue of disparagement and condemnation; they encompassed a rich diversity of opinions and perspectives, some of which were favourably disposed to eastern cultures and hostile to imperialism. The extensive incorporation into British culture of eastern fashions belied the notion that the west held only contempt for the east, and demands more thorough empirical research into western cultural views, rather than abstract theorising. Mackenzie's criticisms were not well received, and elicited a vitriolic response.

Others have attacked Said and his followers on similar grounds. Linda Colley, in particular has pointed out that contrary to Said, western reactions to Islam 'were never homogenous or monolithic'.[23] She demonstrates that attitudes towards Muslim powers in the Mediterranean world varied over time and geography, and were quite favourable before the mid-eighteenth century. In this world, it was other Christian European powers who presented the principal threat to British interests, while British possessions such as Gibraltar and Minorca were dependent upon trade with the Muslim kingdoms of North Africa for essential provisions. Said's depiction of a largely uniform Christian perspective on the Islamic world is thus seen as an oversimplification. Bayly reinforces the criticism of this 'retrogressive' tendency in post-colonial thinking, pointing instead to the diversity and 'long-standing debates among Europeans' about the nature of the non-European world.[24] David Washbrook, Reader in South Asian History at St Antony's College, Oxford, takes a different tack in his critique of post-colonial theory.[25] Said emphasised the powerful influence of Enlightenment rationalism in western thought, which asserted that there are universal truths which can be discovered through the application of reason. The upshot was that once such absolute truths were revealed, traditional and irrational beliefs and behaviours would have no place in the world. From there it was a small step for the western Enlightenment thinkers in the eighteenth and nineteenth centuries to conclude that the technological and economic leadership of the west reflected the superiority of its rationally based culture, and that therefore all traditional non-western cultures were inferior, false and rightly destined to be bulldozed by the relentless march of western reason. Oriental cultures were not only second-rate; they were also destined to be supplanted by that of the west. But Washbrook rejects this as a very partial reading of western cultural development. European Romanticism rejected many aspects of the Enlightenment, and postulated far more sympathetic interpretations of non-European cultures.[26] In this respect, European culture and its perceptions of the non-European world were more diverse, pluralistic and subject to change over time, than post-colonial theory allows.

Washbrook also challenges the notion in post-colonial theory that European cultural responses to the rest of the globe were uniform. They were neither as consistent, nor as divorced from the reality of local societies and cultures as has been claimed. The European focus upon caste as a defining social entity in India, and the tribe in Africa, were not figments of the European imagination, but founded on indigenous perceptions and realities. Washbrook contends that the success of the British in securing effective collaborators in these societies bears testament to the basic accuracy of at least some of their ideas about the non-European world into which they were moving.[27] Moreover, the collaborative relationships which allowed the British in many instances to assert themselves with a minimum of coercive force rested upon the existence of common ideas about the indigenous society which were shared by local collaborating elites. Thus colonialist perceptions of non-European cultures were much more than mere projections of western prejudices or imagination. From here, Washbrook moves onto a very telling criticism of Said's work. By reducing western culture to a simplified or 'essentialised' model of Enlightenment rationalism, Said effectively commits the same crimes of misrepresentation, objectification and devaluation he attributes to western treatments of the east. In response to the travesty of western 'orientalism', Said offers an equally demeaning 'occidentalism.[28]

Post-colonial theory more generally is attacked by 'orthodox' imperial historians for its abandonment not only of historical method, but also of systematic analysis of colonial societies and ordinary people whose contacts with European imperial rulers were minimal. Subaltern studies tend to focus upon the lives of those in the indigenous society who dealt directly with the European governors, to the exclusion of the masses who rarely encountered the bearers of imperial power. As a result, the impact of empire on the lives of ordinary people disappears from view, together with any consideration of such questions of economic exploitation, poverty or the imperial legacy for economic development. Washbrook attributes this to a form of elitism, noting the upper-class credentials of many post-colonial theorists from the former colonies. He chides subaltern studies for ignoring the plight of the Indian peasantry under British rule in favour of giving vent to 'the angst of the Calcutta intelligentsia'.[29] Marxist historians particularly criticise the abandonment of analysis of class structures and relations of economic power.[30] Kennedy denounces the 'dubious if not delusional' notion held by elitist post-colonial writers that the oppression of the west can be overthrown by writing obscure tracts for almost exclusively academic western audiences.[31] The acidity of such comments originates in a general exasperation at both the written style of post-colonial theory, and its presumption in rejecting the methods and extensive body of work on imperialism built up by historians. Kennedy mocks the 'clotted', jargon-laden prose of colonial discourse, echoing the call of another disgruntled historian for a 'devil's dictionary of cultural studies'.[32] But his most round criticism is for those post-colonial texts which most blatantly ignore the principles of historical analysis.[33]

Perhaps partly because of this barrage of criticism, some recent writing in colonial discourse has sought to embrace historical method, and has significantly amended the notion of a monolithic western cultural image of the colonial 'other'. The collection of essays in Codell and Macleod's *Orientalism Transposed* seeks to explore the complex ways in which the colonised sometimes subverted western stereotypes of themselves, sometimes applying the same stereotypes to the British.[34] They also examine how British culture itself was shaped by contact with the empire, and how experience of one colony shaped British cultural responses to another. From this emerge much more diverse images of British cultural interpretation of empire, 'that fracture Said's monolithic Orientalism into multiple instabilities and complexities of colonial discourse'.[35] Leonard Bell's essay in particular demonstrates how the work of British artists in the 1820s was profoundly altered by experience of empire, questioning 'the notion of a unified, monolithic western "imperial eye"'.[36] Dianne Sachko Macleod demonstrates how some Victorian women adopted Turkish Ottoman dress to assert their independence and resistance to British patriarchy.[37] Overall, the essays substantially reject the notion of a single western cultural perception of empire, replacing it with a much more diverse and fluid model, in which a continuing process of interaction between the cultures of metropole and colonies perpetually changed western ideas of their subject nations, throwing up new ideas which substantially altered western culture itself. It will be seen in the next chapter that this idea appears again in the work of Catherine Hall on British cultural responses to their West Indian colonies.

Specific work on British India has also produced important revisions of post-colonial theory. E. M. Collingham's *Imperial Bodies* seeks to chart the shifting British experience and perceptions of India through changing British notions of the appropriate treatment and dressing of the body in the alien Indian environment.[38] Collingham shows how in the eighteenth century, far from rejecting oriental customs, the British opted for an 'Indianised body', with the wearing of Indian clothes, exposure to the Indian environment to strengthen resistance to disease, and the consumption of Indian spicy foods. Social and sexual intercourse with Indians was regarded as acceptable, and even to be encouraged. The *Nautch*, a social event involving music and dancing girls, became a particularly popular meeting place for Europeans and Indians.[39] Collingham argues that this ready acceptance of Indian social norms was displaced during the nineteenth century by a more overtly racist and separatist regime for the body. By the 1830s, the black heavy cloth suit had become the standard dress of the British male in India, while Indian food was increasingly rejected in favour of imported tinned English provisions. The Indian environment increasingly came to be regarded as dangerously hostile, from which the body had to be isolated and protected. This 'Anglicisation' of the body necessitated minimal contact with Indians, which was generally restricted to servants and officials. Social contact was increasingly curtailed, and sexual liaisons across the racial divide became unacceptable. British living quarters and districts were sharply segregated from Indian ones, and every effort was made to make them islands of Britishness. British neighbourhoods came to resemble idealised versions of English country villages, based on a rose tinted fantasy image of the home country. Collingham's work is important because it implies significant change and evolution in British perceptions of India and Indian culture, a tendency which runs contrary to the consistency of attitudes over time suggested in Said's work. Other contributions reinforce this analysis. William Dalrymple's study of Anglo-Indian relations in the eighteenth century supports Collingham's picture of cross cultural exchange during that period.[40] Dalrymple's (b. 1967) distinguished career as a travel writer with several books and television series on modern India in the 1990s led him into the history of Anglo-Indian relations. The result was a best-selling popular work on late eighteenth century India, the success of which demonstrates the extent to which the debate about culture and empire has seeped into the popular consciousness. The relationship and marriage of Major James Achilles Kirkpatrick, the British Resident at Hyderabad from 1798 to 1805, to Khair Un Nissa, an Indian *begum* (Muslim noble woman) is the main focus of Dalrymple's book, but he emphasises that it was just one of numerous examples of inter-racial relationships which involved mutual acceptance of both cultures. Like Collingham, Dalrymple sees racism and segregation as a development of the nineteenth century, although the first signs of it were already apparent in official disapproval of Kirkpatrick's union. Dalrymple cites Said's work as an example of a tendency to ignore this earlier phase of cultural interchange and mutual appreciation. 'It was as if', writes Dalrymple, 'this early promiscuous mingling of races and ideas, modes of dress and ways of living, was something that was on no-one's agenda and suited nobody's version of events'.[41]

Just as post-colonial writing has started to embrace historical method, so mainstream imperial historians have ventured more enthusiastically into the territory of culture and empire. The result has also been a significant revision of Said's 'monolith' of enduring western cultural evaluations of the colonised 'other'. Linda Colley's *Captives* is one of the most interesting recent explorations of British cultural attitudes to empire, and offers a complex picture of values which both changed over time and varied in accordance with the social origins of the British observer.[42] Colley (b. 1949), whose career has encompassed spells at LSE, Yale and Princeton, has recently emerged as a major contributor to the debate about the British empire. Married to David Cannadine, who has also published on British imperialism, Colley's earlier work focused on the emergence of the British national identity in the eighteenth century. It was this wider concern with nationalism which seems to have led Colley into the study of the cultural interaction between the British and the peoples with whom empire brought them into contact. Colley herself has admitted that the explosion in interest in imperialism and culture in the 1980s helped her overcome her rather negative undergraduate experience of imperial history as a 'comprehensively masculine enterprise' preoccupied with the affairs of the conquering power.[43]

A central theme in *Captives* is that the British were never quite as powerful as the vastness of their empire suggested. Limited in manpower and resources in their tiny homeland, the British were rarely as confident as their swaggering imperial bombast implied. In fact one of the most common encounters for Britons with the non-European 'other', both within and without the empire, was as their prisoner or captive. Colley explores three theatres of British operations where such experiences became commonplace; the north African coast of the Mediterranean in the sixteenth and seventeenth centuries (dominated by Muslim powers and the 'Barbary pirates'), the colonies of North America in the eighteenth century, and India in the eighteenth and early nineteenth centuries. On the first of these, Colley argues that British responses to Islam were very different from those depicted in Said's work. Far from arrogant disdain, former British captives of the north African Muslim regimes reported their formidable power, and instilled in their countrymen a certain awe and respect for Islamic might.[44] Moreover, British relations with these states were by no means consistently hostile. The British outposts on Minorca and Gibraltar became dependent upon the North African Muslim regimes for essential supplies, and as such the Muslims were not the principal enemy. That status was accorded to the rival Christian powers of Spain and France, whose power, ambition and Roman Catholicism rendered them a much greater threat in Protestant, British eyes. Colley contends that for all their fear and hostility towards Islam, European Catholic rivals were frequently regarded as a far more dangerous 'other', even to the point of comparing Islam favourably with Catholicism.[45] Moreover, Colley argues that this ambivalent perception of Islam persisted even into the nineteenth century, checking any notion that the Muslim world was there for the taking.[46]

Colley's analysis of the British presence in the North American states also concludes that British perceptions of non-white ethnic groups do not easily fit into the pigeon hole allocated to them by post-colonial theorists. Contact and friction with native Americans in the seventeenth and eighteenth centuries was frequently interpreted very differently by the colonists on the frontier, and domestic opinion in Britain. Whereas the adage 'the only good Indian is a dead one' summarised the perspective of many of those in the colonies whose views had been shaped by experiences of conflict and captives' tales of Indian savagery, domestic British opinion was more ambivalent, perceiving the native Americans as victims of white colonists' greed for land, despite their acknowledged brutality.[47] Towards the end of the eighteenth century of course, the white colonists themselves became the problem, as dissatisfaction with the terms of British rule deteriorated into revolution and war. Colley explains how the weakness of the British position in the colonies and their limited military strength, forced them to look to ethnic groups such as native Americans and blacks for support. For the British authorities, the American empire was a hybrid entity, in which the differing interests of native Americans, white colonists and blacks had to be somehow reconciled It was not simply a question of giving the whites everything they desired.[48] For their part, native Americans and blacks correctly perceived that attitudes towards them among the white colonists were far more hostile than those emanating from London. Continuing British imperial government seemed to offer greater security than the prospect of unfettered rule by land-hungry and hostile white colonists, and so they tended to fight on London's side. As Colley puts it, this was 'one more demonstration of how empire, so often assumed now to be *necessarily* racist in operation and ethos, could sometimes be conspicuously poly-ethnic in quality and policy, because it had to be'.[49]

British experiences in India in the century after the battle of Plassey were also characterised by a sense of vulnerability and a need to accommodate oriental values. Colley notes the large numbers of white British troops captured by the various regional states in their wars with the East India Company. Tipu Sultan of Mysore's forces not only defeated the Company on several occasions, they also took several thousand British troops captive, a sizeable proportion of the white British forces in India which numbered no more than 10,000 at the time.[50] The fact was that the British were few and heavily dependent upon Indian collaborators, not least the thousands of sepoys who formed the majority of British forces on the sub-continent. This compelled the British authorities to temper any tendency to contempt for Indians, while heightening their impatience with their own soldiery, drawn from the poorest ranks of British society. Colley describes the miserable condition of the British troops in India, who were segregated from local society, lest they contaminate it with their unruly ways. Disease-ridden and subject to the savage discipline of the East India Company's army, they frequently rebelled, deserted or engaged in drink-fuelled anti-social behaviour. At a time when revolution in France, and the social upheaval of industrialisation at home were heightening British middle and upper class fears of the poorest classes in British society, these problems led the British authorities in India to see their troops as more alien and 'other' than the Indians.[51] Thus Governor General William Bentinck in 1835 abolished the use of flogging to discipline Indian sepoys, but retained it for European troops.[52] In the early nineteenth century at least, British troops were demonised as much as Indians – they were, in Colley's phrase, 'the subalterns with white faces'.[53]

British power increased as the nineteenth century progressed, in spite of a major setback in Afghanistan in the 1840s. The development of new technologies of warfare gave them a decisive edge over local Indian powers on the battlefield. The upshot was the emergence of more arrogant and confident British attitudes to Indians, which hardened significantly in the middle decades of the century because of the rebellion of 1857. However, Colley's point is that British rule in India and elsewhere, compared to other empires, was peculiarly vulnerable to rebellion principally because of constraints on resources. As a result, the British were always very dependent upon collaborating elites within their empire, a contingency which required them to adopt a far more inclusive ideology towards their subject peoples than is suggested by most post-colonial theory. In Colley's words, the empire had always been a 'cross-cultural enterprise', most notably in India.[54] As a result, Said's notion that the British and other western powers had long nurtured a sense of superiority over non-European cultures is a gross oversimplification of evolving British ideological responses to the wider world. Long-standing limitations on British resources and power, the need to recruit non-European allies in acquiring and securing the empire, and the changing nature of British society itself were all factors which helped produce a constantly evolving and fluid cultural response to empire. In addition, the socially diverse British agents on the imperial frontier, and the extreme variations in local environments, cultures and circumstances which prevailed there, suggests that the repertoire of British responses to the non-European world was too wide to be categorised as a single cultural perspective. Nonetheless, Colley believes that these shifting British cultural interpretations of the empire were important in shaping both its growth and governing strategies. In this respect at least, the cultural emphasis of post-colonial theory has influenced Colley's analysis of British imperial development.

However, perhaps the most original response to the new interest in imperialist culture has come in David Cannadine's *Ornamentalism*.[55] Brought up in Birmingham, Cannadine (b. 1950) emerged in the 1980s and 1990s as an eminent transAtlantic historian, like his wife, Linda Colley. Following spells at Cambridge and Columbia universities, Cannadine became head of the prestigious Institute of Historical Research in London in 1998. There were parallels in the development of Cannadine's and Colley's interests in British imperialism. Both came under the powerful influence of Professor John Plumb of Christ's College, Cambridge in the 1970s, and were infected with his enthusiasm for British social history. They both confessed to a muted aware-ness of empire in their youth, which coincided with imperial decolonisation.[56] Like Colley, it was Cannadine's preoccupation with British society which led him into British imperial history.

Cannadine came to the British empire as an eminent historian of the British aristocracy.[57] As such he was well placed to analyse attitudes to the empire among the elite who governed it. In his introduction, Cannadine argues that to understand the British cultural response to empire, it is first necessary to appreciate the prevailing obsession with class and hierarchy which dominated British culture and society, and he directs his readers to his book *Class in Britain* which is intended to be a companion to *Ornamentalism*.[58] Focusing on the period from 1850 to the 1950s, Cannadine rejects Said's notion that the prevailing theme in British cultural perceptions of their subject peoples was based solely on a sense of their difference, inferiority or 'otherness'.[59] Instead, Britons also sought out cultural and social similarities with Britain in the colonies, in their efforts to make sense of what were alien and sometimes intimidating social environments. Cannadine does not deny that the British, like all western powers, regarded themselves as more civilised and racially superior to the peoples they conquered, but he contends that this was only one facet of their mental construction of indigenous colonial soci-eties.[60] The bewilderment, alienation and occasional fear which accompanied personal encounters of the imperial periphery were alleviated by seeking out points of familiarity and similarity with home. Cannadine argues that to understand how this shaped British perceptions of their subject peoples, it is first necessary to grasp the dominance of hierarchy and class in the society from which the British came. British society consisted of finely layered strata of social classes, each with their defining codes of behav-iour, language, dress and customs, which provided the individual with a strong sense of place and purpose. At the top were the aris-tocracy, whose cultural values and tastes were deemed to be the pinnacle of civilised achievement, and were imitated by all who aspired to power and social elevation.

It followed that British colonial servants tended to look for similar traits in the local societies which they were attempting to rule. Colonial Governors and senior officials, who themselves were frequently drawn from the ranks of the aristocracy, sought to identify local elites with whom they could empathise. In an empire which depended extensively upon the collaboration of local elites to minimise the costs of governance, there were powerful practical incentives to cultivate such relations, rather than allow attitudes of racial superiority to generate enmity.[61] Cannadine makes the point that British policy in such tropical colonies as Malaya and the African possessions came to be guided by Lord Lugard's notion of the 'dual mandate', of protecting traditional social and political structures by governing through them.[62] In the twentieth century, as domestic change in Britain began to erode the social hierarchy to which colonial officials referred as their model of the 'good society', defending the traditional order of colonial societies took on a new urgency for those who bemoaned the passing of the old order. There were even efforts to replicate an idealised version of traditional rural British society. Cannadine refers particularly to the fashion for building medieval style baronial halls and stately homes in the colonies. The viceregal lodge at Simla in India, was just one such example.[63] Such efforts to display a traditional British social image echoed the stress on defending local social cultures and social orders. There were numerous examples of protecting traditional structures. In the Malay states, the local Sultans continued their positions as ceremonial heads of state, although the British Residents whose role was supposed to be purely advisory came to exercise the real power. In the princely states of India British Residents enjoyed similar relationships with the various Maharajahs and Nizams in whose name they exercised power. During the late nineteenth and early twentieth centuries, similar arrangements sprang up across the African colonies.

Every effort was made to prop up the status and dignity of the local ruler, even if real power had been usurped by ostensibly deferential British advisers. In the Malay states, the Sultans enjoyed vast personal wealth and spectacular displays of ceremonial pomp, to underline their status and importance. Cannadine uses an extensive range of colonial photographs to bring out the use of ceremony as a 'cement' to bind the empire together. A recurring image is of the local ruler or dignitary appearing before the crowds in his full traditional regalia, together with his British adviser decked in his own lesser garb of imperial splendour. Cannadine shows how the honours system was employed to recognise the eminence of local leaders. For example, three special orders of chivalry were established for India in the late nineteenth century: The Most Exalted Order of the Star of India established in 1861, the Most Eminent Order of the Indian Empire (1878) and the Imperial Order of the Crown of India (1878).[64] These were awarded to both Indians and Britons, and were intended to signify that empire was a cross-racial enterprise, in which the efforts of all would be recognised. Both the imperial civil servant and the local leader could be equally honoured. This device was intended to do more than merely reward collaborators. It also incorporated 'native' dignitaries into an elaborate hierarchy of honours, at the summit of which was the British monarch. In this way the symbols of aristocracy, honours and monarchy were used as a unifying cultural mechanism, drawing together British officials and local elites all over the empire into a sense of common imperial enterprise, at the head of which was the British queen or king. Pomp, ceremony, medals, honours, ritual – the baubles of empire – collectively amounted in Cannadine's words to *Ornamentalism*, empire and 'hierarchy made visible, immanent and actual'.[65] Perhaps the most powerful ceremonial expression of this was the great Coronation *Durbar* of 1911 in Delhi, at which King George V and his Queen received homage from the Indian princes. The spectacular ceremonial splendour was designed to inspire awe and to express a unity between governors and governed, in which Indian rulers were accorded due recognition and respect for their place in the imperial hierarchy headed by the British King-Emperor.[66]

Of course, race remained a source of division within the empire, and white supremacist attitudes permeated all relations between the British and their subject peoples. The inhabitants of the colonies of white settlement received preferential treatment because of their ethnic origins, thus the granting of a significant measure of self government to Canada, New Zealand and Australia during the course of the nineteenth century. Cannadine makes the point that the honours system and the cultivation of local hierarchies and elites also operated here, and served to instil a sense of belonging to the wider empire. Non-white subjects, however, were unequivocally regarded as inferior and requiring the benefits of more direct rule and guidance from above. But Cannadine notes that considerations of class and hierarchy some-times created confusion for the British on questions of race. The high social status of a non-white representative of the local elite occasionally superseded considerations of ethnicity. Frequently they were regarded by patrician colonial officials as superior to whites of modest social origins, though such judgements were usually held in confidence. In the 1870s, the wife of Arthur Hamilton Gordon, Governor of Fiji commented upon the good manners and fine breeding of high-ranking Fijian ladies, adding that her (white) 'Nurse can't understand it at all, she looks down on them as an inferior race. I don't like to tell her that these ladies are my equals while she is not!'.[67] While generally people of different race were regarded as inferior, high social status could sometimes challenge or negate this general categorisation, particularly among the highest ranks. Cannadine offers a compelling anecdote to illustrate the occasional confusion caused when class contradicted race. In 1881, King Kalakaua of Hawaii attended a party in England organised by Lady Spencer. In atten-dance were several Royal personages, including the Prince of Wales (the future Edward VII) and Wilhelm, the German Crown Prince and future Kaiser. The Prince of Wales insisted that as a King, Kalakaua should take precedence over the German crown prince in matters of ceremonial etiquette. Edward's response to Wilhelm's objection to this arrangement captured the dilemma about race and class in the now unacceptable racist language of the day: 'Either the brute is a king, or he's a common or garden nigger; and if the latter, what's he doing here?'[68]

The thrust of Cannadine's argument is that the British cultural response to the non-European 'other' was far more complex than much post-colonial theory allows. British attitudes to social hierarchy, the need for effective local collaborators and an inclusive ideology which could bind the empire together, all mitigated the harsh racism which pervaded British imperial culture. Moreover, Cannadine contends that when the British empire was eventually dissolved, a transcontinental social order began to disappear with it; one which had embraced a far more sophisticated set of inter-racial relations than has been recognised.[69] Ultimately, the British obsession with social hierarchy was as important a determining factor as race in the development of the British empire.

Critical responses to Cannadine's thesis are still emerging. One problem is that not all prominent imperial figures were drawn into Cannadine's inclusive ornamentalist network, even on the British side. Such eminent figures as Joseph Chamberlain, Rudyard Kipling and Cecil Rhodes never received the imperial honours so central to Cannadine's system. Moreover, Cannadine's focus very much reflects his earlier academic preoccupation with the aristocracy. Very few imperial actors of lower rank appear in his analysis.[70] The most glaring omission, on both sides of the racial divide, are the men of commerce, the merchants and capitalists whose cross-cultural/racial relations were so important for the economic health of empire. Up to the 1830s, these commercial relations were often closer and more intense than those at the lofty heights of colonial government, based as they were on mutual material self-interest. They probably had a much more important role in shaping cultural relations between rulers and ruled than Cannadine acknowledges.[71] Moreover, as Maria Misra demonstrates, leading figures in the Calcutta managing agency houses adopted far more trenchant and racist attitudes than did British officialdom in India.[72] In this respect, she cautions against claims that British attitudes on race were in any sense homogenous. But this criticism is not applicable to Cannadine alone. Said, and other post-colonial writers seldom seem to focus upon the mundane yet important day-to-day relations between British and indigenous merchants, preferring the more grandiose but distant pronouncements of senior officials and the literati. Another important area of work neglected by Cannadine and others is that of intelligence gathering. Bayly's work on the development of intelligence networks in India under the East India Company suggests that British contacts with Indian society were far richer and more complex than is evident in much of the writing reviewed in this chapter.[73] Without doubt there is much work to be done in unravelling the routine interactions between British imperial and indigenous actors on the periphery at all levels, before a fuller picture of cross cultural relations within the British empire will emerge.

Clearly these attempts to construct over-arching theories of empire and culture have influenced a generation of imperial historians and post-colonial theorists in the decades since *Orientalism*. If all have been found wanting in some respects, it is clear that they have at least focused attention on a previously neglected aspect of imperialism, namely the contemporary perceptions of empire and the peoples within them, held by conquerors and conquered alike. They also wrested the study of imperialism from the grasp of the economic and political historians who had dominated the subject since the late nineteenth century. As a result, historical writing on British imperial history is now richer and more dynamic than ever. As will be seen in the next chapter, the flourishing of post-colonial theory, and the responses of historians to it has generated an expanding literature on particular aspects of imperial cultural relations, particularly those concerned with religion, race, gender, class and popular culture.

Notes

1 See, for example: F. de Saussure, *Course in General Linguistics* (London, 1974); Roland Barthes, *Elements of Semiology* (London, 1967); Claude Levi-Strauss, *Structural Anthropology* (London, 1968).
2 J. Derrida, *Writing and Difference* (London, 1978).
3 M. Foucault, *Discipline and Punish* (Harmondsworth, 1979).
4 For a sense of the range of Kiernan's work on imperialism, see the compilation of his essays, H. J. Kaye (ed.), *Imperialism and its Contradictions* (New York, 1995).
5 Originally entitled *The Lords of Human Kind: Black Man, Yellow Man and White Man in the Age of Empire* (New York, 1969), a second edition was published twenty-six years later under a slightly revised title: V. Kiernan, *The Lords of Human Kind: European Attitudes to Other Cultures in the Imperial Age* (New York, 1995). All references are to this later edition.
6 *Ibid.*, p. 333.
7 *Ibid.*, p. 332.
8 *Ibid.*, p. 338.
9 E. Said, *Culture and Imperialism* (London, 1994), p. 60.
10 E. Said, *Orientalism* (London, 1978).

11 Said, *Culture and Imperialism*.

12 C. A. Bayly, 'The second British empire', in R. W. Winks (ed.) *The Oxford History of the British Empire Vol V: Historiography* (Oxford, 1999), pp. 54–72; p. 68

13 D. Kennedy, 'Imperial history and post-colonial theory', *The Journal of Imperial and Commonwealth History* 24:3 (September 1996), 345–63; 346.

14 E. Said, *Orientalism* pp. 59–61.

15 *Ibid.*, pp. 31–3.

16 E. Said, *Culture and Imperialism* p. 61.

17 See Ranajit Guha, 'On aspects of the historiography of colonial India', in R. Guha (ed.), *Subaltern Studies I. Writings on South Asian History and Society* (Delhi, 1982); R. O'Hanlon, '"Recovering the subject", subaltern studies and histories of resistance in colonial South Asia', *Modern Asian Studies* 12:1 (1988), 189–224.

18 G. Chakravorty Spivak, 'Subaltern studies, deconstructing historiography', in R. Guha (ed.), *Subaltern Studies IV* (Delhi, 1985); R. Young, *White Mythologies: Writing History and the West* (London, 1990), chs 1 and 2.

19 A. Nandy, *The Intimate Enemy: Loss and Recovery of Self under Colonialism* (Delhi, 1983).

20 C. Midgley, *Gender and Imperialism* (Manchester, 1998); D. Chakrabarty, *Rethinking Working Class History: Bengal 1890–1940* (Princeton, 1989).

21 J. Mackenzie, *Orientalism: History, Theory and the Arts* (Manchester, 1995). For further discussion of Mackenzie's work see p. 163

22 *Ibid.*, pp. 214–15.

23 Colley, *Captives*, p. 102.

24 C. A. Bayly, 'The second British empire', p. 70.

25 D. Washbrook, 'Orients and occidents: colonial discourse theory and the historiography of the British empire', in Winks (ed.), *The Oxford History of the British Empire Vol V: Historiography*, pp. 596–611.

26 *Ibid.*, p. 603.

27 *Ibid.*, p. 604.

28 *Ibid.*, p. 606.

29 *Ibid.*, p. 608.

30 A. Ahmad, *In Theory: Classes, Nations and Literatures* (London, 1992).

31 Kennedy, 'Imperial history and post-colonial theory', pp. 349–50.

32 *Ibid.*, p. 349.

33 *Ibid.*, pp. 351–2.

34 J. F. Codell and D. S. Macleod, *Orientalism Transposed: The Impact of the Colonies on British Culture* (Aldershot, 1998), p. 3.

35 *Ibid.*, pp. 5–6.

36 L. Bell, 'To see or not to see: conflicting eyes in the travel art of Augustus Earle', in Codell and Macleod (eds) *Orientalism Transposed*, pp. 117–39; p. 130.

37 D. S. Macleod, 'Cross-cultural cross-dressing: class, gender and modernist sexual identity', in *Orientalism Transposed*, pp. 63–85.

38 E. M. Collingham, *Imperial Bodies: The Physical Experience of the Raj c. 1800–1947* (Cambridge, 2001).

39 *Ibid.*, ch. 1, 'The Indianized Body'.

40 W. Dalrymple, *White Mughals: Love and Betrayal in Eighteenth Century India* (London, 2002).

41 *Ibid.*, p. xli.

42 L. Colley, *Captives: Britain, Empire and the World 1600–1850* (London, 2003).

43 L. Colley, 'What is imperial history now?', in D. Cannadine (ed.), *What is History Now* (London, 2002), pp. 132–47; pp. 132–3.

44 L. Colley, *Captives*, pp. 125–6.

45 *Ibid.*, p. 125.

46 *Ibid.*, p. 132.

47 *Ibid.*, p. 188.

48 *Ibid.*, p. 234.

49 *Ibid.*, p. 236.

50 *Ibid.*, p. 276.

51 *Ibid.*, pp. 335–40.

52 *Ibid.*, p. 341.

53 *Ibid.*, p. 316.

54 *Ibid.*, pp. 371–2.

55 D. Cannadine, *Ornamentalism: How the British Saw Their Empire* (London, 2001).

56 *Ibid.*, p. 198.

57 See D. Cannadine, *The Decline and Fall of the British Aristocracy* (London, 1990).

58 D. Cannadine, *Class in Britain* (London, 2000).

59 Cannadine, *Ornamentalism*, p. xix.

60 *Ibid.*, p. 5.

61 *Ibid.*, pp. 58–9.

62 *Ibid.*, p. 62.

63 *Ibid.*, p. 50.

64 *Ibid.*, p. 88.

65 *Ibid.*, p. 122.

66 *Ibid.*, pp. 53–4.

67 *Ibid.*, p. 59.

68 *Ibid.*, p. 8.

69 *Ibid.*, pp. 153–4.

70 See J. Mackenzie, 'Prejudice behind the pomp and baubles' (a review of *Ornamentalism*) in the *Times Higher Education Supplement*, 27 July 2001.

71 See A. Webster, 'An early global business in a colonial context: the strategies, management and failure of John Palmer and Company of Calcutta', *Enterprise and Society: The International Journal of Business History* 6:1 (March 2005), 98–133.

72 M. Misra, *Business, Race and Politics in British India c1850–1960* (Oxford, 1999), pp. 8–10.

73 C. A. Bayly, 'Knowing the country: empire and information in India', in *Modern Asian Studies* 27:1 (1993), 3–43; C. A. Bayly, *Empire and Information: Intelligence Gathering and Social Communication in India 1780–1870* (Cambridge, 1996).

6

Cultural explanations of British imperialism II: religion, race, gender and class

The emergence of post-colonial theory in the late 1970s, and responses to it during the years which followed, helped inspire extensive work on specific aspects of culture and imperialism. Wider social and academic developments also encouraged this new interest in imperial culture. The rise of immigrant communities and cultures in Britain and Europe from former colonies in the 1960s inspired interest in earlier encounters between metropolitan and colonial societies and value systems. Violent racist responses to immigration in Britain and elsewhere led to liberal fears of a resurgence of the far-right political movements which had plunged Europe into the Second World War. Such concerns prompted historians to seek the origins of racist attitudes in the imperial experience. At the same time, other social and intellectual trends encouraged closer engagement with the cultural aspects of imperialism. The decline of religion and changes in the social structure of post-war Britain had coincided with the deconstruction of empire, suggesting that imperialism may have been instrumental in sustaining the traditional social order and value system. The rise of interdisciplinary studies in British polytechnics and colleges of higher education in the early 1960s, closely followed by the emergence of cultural studies in British universities, also encouraged and legitimised a new preoccupation with empire as a formative agency in the development of British and colonial societies and cultures.

As a result, new fields of imperial history began to be mapped out from the late 1960s and 1970s. The role of organised religion in the spread and consolidation of empire was one important area of study, particularly the role of missionaries at the frontier of empire and in newly acquired colonies. Another theme was the justifications for empire which emerged from the evolving debate about race and civilisation in the late eighteenth and nineteenth centuries. The burgeoning interest in feminist history and gender studies inevitably turned to questions of gender and sexual relations in the colonies, both within and across ethnic boundaries. These focused upon the effects upon imperial governance and colonial societies of cross-ethnic relations between the sexes, and the rise of a substantial white female population in the dependent, non-white empire. Another area of interest was the question of how Britain's emerging class system interacted with empire, an issue already touched upon in the earlier analysis of Cannadine's *ornamentalism* thesis. The emergence of an organised and increasingly literate working class in the late Victorian period meant that the empire became a subject of mass interest and scrutiny. How could empire, with its costs and sacrifices, be sold to an increasingly confident and democratised mass population? New explorations of Victorian popular culture in Britain, therefore, opened fresh avenues of enquiry. The development of the music hall, popular press and other forms of mass media, which promoted and justified the British empire began to attract historical investigation. The introduction of mass education and the widening of the franchise by the Reform Acts of 1867 and 1884 created a new, democratic mass culture in which politicians and pro-imperial interests found it necessary to justify their pro-imperial policies to a widening and increasingly politically conscious electorate. This chapter will explore the historical debate about these aspects of British imperialism.

Among the earlier interpretations of British imperial expansion, Hobson expressed perhaps the clearest view of the relationship between religion and the British empire. He saw Christian missionaries at home and on the frontier as ideological advocates of empire because it offered the prospect of a secure environment in which to make converts. As such they were merely one of a coterie of British interests (financiers, army officers, arms manufacturers) who constituted the main driving force behind imperial expansion.[1] This perception of missionaries as agents of empire on the frontier reappeared in the work of J. S.

Galbraith, who depicted them as one of several destabilising presences on the 'turbulent' imperial frontier which frequently precipitated British forward movement.[2] In fact, this tendency to connect the activities of church and missions in the less developed world with imperialism, was until recently a common theme in many accounts of empire. Among historians from former colonies, this view became particularly strong. Case studies in Africa suggested that missionaries became progressively more racist under British imperial rule. Missionaries came to be seen as promoters of both imperial expansion and white supremacism, in effect the ideological wing of empire.[3]

As Professor Norman Etherington of the University of western Australia points out however, the study of the relations between Christianity, churches, missions and empire is a relatively underdeveloped sphere of scholarship which attracted only the passing interest of imperial historians for much of the twentieth century.[4] Nonetheless, new interpretations have emerged which challenge this predominantly negative picture of Christianity's role in empire. It has been noted, for example, that missionary philosophies varied from sect to sect. The established Anglican Church established bishoprics in the colonies (especially North America) with the support of the British government to meet the needs of white settlers. But its approach to spreading the word differed profoundly from other denominations. For example, in the late eighteenth and early nineteenth centuries the nonconformist churches adopted a much more aggressive policy of proselytisation than the Anglicans who, as agents of the established church, were much more constrained by colonial authorities wary of the unpredictable consequences of widespread conversions.[5] In contrast, the establishment of the various nonconformist missionary organisations such as the Baptist Missionary Society (1792) and the London Missionary Society (1796) signalled a determination to take the Christian God to the heathen masses of the empire. The variation in approach adopted by different sects has contributed to revisions of the orthodox stereotype of the racist and imperialist missionary. For one thing, many of those central to missionary work were not white Britons, but converts of different colour. In this process of 'indigenising' missionary work, the meanings of Christian teachings were subtly but fundamentally altered, sometimes incorporating aspects of local religious belief. Christian ideology was thereby frequently transformed into a tool for criticising imperial oppression, and a medium through which subject races could articulate demands and grievances.[6] Moreover, it has been argued that the varying impact of missionary work on colonial or less developed societies owes more to conditions and circumstances than the efforts or intentions of the missionaries themselves. The enduring strength of local religions and cultures hindered even the most enthusiastic missions, particularly in the Indian sub-continent, where Hinduism and Islam presented formidable barriers to spreading the word. The existence of social outcast groups, however, particularly in the lower Hindu castes, proved to be fertile ground for missionary work, eventually yielding millions of Christian converts in the lower reaches of Indian society.[7] Etherington highlights missionary case studies in the South Pacific and South Africa, which show that the destabilisation of local societies by war or other events sometimes created widespread feelings of insecurity and greater openness to missionary appeals for conversion.[8] All of these studies point to the evolution and impact of missionary churches being determined as much by local conditions and agents as by the prejudices, plans and actions of white missionaries arriving from the metropole.

Thus the debate about the role and impact of missionary churches in the British empire has centred upon questions of whether or not missionaries and their teachings promoted or ameliorated imperialism, and the relative importance of local circumstances and missionaries as against ideas and personnel imported from Britain, in determining the character of the missionary churches in the colonies. Case studies of missionaries in particular colonies have been the main forum for this discourse, with few attempts to try to draw a more generalised picture of missionary impact across the empire. Given the huge variation in cultural, social and economic circumstances within the empire, this was inevitable and necessary, though it has tended to make it difficult to draw generalisations about the role and impact of missionaries. The most notable exception to this has been the work of Andrew Porter, whose 1993 article in the *Journal of Imperial and Commonwealth History* has been particularly influential[9]. Porter (b. 1945) is an important figure in British imperial history. Rhodes Professor of Imperial History at King's College London since 1993, and for some years editor of *The Journal of Imperial and Commonwealth History*, much of Porter's earlier work was concerned with British imperialism in southern Africa in the late nineteenth century. In the early 1990s, his focus switched to the role of religion and missionaries in the empire.

Porter makes a number of important points. In particular, he considers the extent to which missionaries contributed to the expansion of the British empire in the 'long' nineteenth century. He concludes that there was certainly a relationship between imperialism and missionary activity but not the one frequently claimed. Porter rejects the tendency of many historians to dismiss early nineteenth-century evangelical missionary beliefs as the mere product of emerging British capitalism, or the unwitting agents of imperialist expansion. For Porter religious belief was characterised by passion, faith and an independence from prevailing capitalist ideology which has been insufficiently emphasised.[10] Moreover, the missionary churches were efficiently organised and capable of asserting their beliefs, especially in the context of nineteenth-century Britain where faith still exercised great purchase on popular opinion. Indeed Porter asserts that the significant missionary impact on the empire stemmed from evangelical Christianity's formidable command of a large section of public opinion in Britain. In this respect, he is slightly critical of the tendency in many local case studies to assert the importance of developments on the periphery over the driving force of missionary proselytisation emanating from the metropole.[11]

From 1750 onwards, the evangelical revival which swept through British Protestantism celebrated the notion that salvation lay in the hands of the believers, rather than intermediaries such as ministers or priests.[12] Individual faith, conscience and action provided the surest road to heaven, and what better way to serve God than by spreading his word across the globe to the ignorant and ungodly? This sense of holy destiny was reinforced by the apparent fitness of British Protestants for the task – did they not represent the most powerful and dynamic nation in the world? Britain's lead in industry, science and exploration all seemed to suggest that her people had been divinely ordained and prepared to perform this task. Porter is unequivocal that this represented a close link between the spread of Christianity and the empire.[13] He notes that between 1780 and 1900, over 120 colonial bishoprics were created, while the 10,000 missionaries active overseas by 1899 were a potent force for spreading ideas of British imperial authority as well as the moral supremacy of Christianity.[14] In addition, the missionaries helped to shape a metropolitan view of the empire and the less developed world which tended to justify imperial expansion. Missionary tales of the degradation, savagery and pitiable ignorance of peoples at the imperial frontier contributed to metropolitan stereotypes and perceptions which convinced many Britons that imperial conquest was frequently an act of humanitarian salvation.[15]

However, Porter dismisses the portrayal of missionaries as either the mere tools of imperial authority or the ruthless purveyors of a doctrine of racial supremacy. He argues that the relationship between missionaries and colonial governments was frequently a difficult one, based on conflict rather than co-operation. Neither the missionary churches nor British governments regarded the other as natural allies. Nonconformist evangelicals, in particular, were deeply suspicious of the British state, in light of its institutional connection with the Anglican establishment. Conversely, British governments saw evangelicalism as a dangerously passionate and wilful movement which had a record of inciting domestic as well as colonial unrest.[16] Missionaries frequently came into conflict with colonial administrators and white settlers, most notably in the West Indies during the 1820s, when they successfully campaigned for an end to slavery.[17] In the early nineteenth century, missionary efforts to convert Indians to Christianity were regarded by some leading officials as a nuisance because they provoked Hindu and Muslim hostility and endangered Anglo–Indian relations.[18] But Porter notes that just as often, relations between missionaries and colonial administrators could be close. Many colonial civil servants were, after all, devout Christians, and this commanded at least some sympathy for the missionary cause. In some contexts, missionaries were regarded as useful, providing vital intelligence from beyond the frontiers of empire, and occasionally constituting a source of influence and authority in their own right. For example, in central and eastern

Africa during the late nineteenth century missionaries were regarded as an important auxiliary to sparsely distributed and under-resourced British colonial administrators.[19] In the view of Sir Harry Johnston, a senior African colonial official, missionaries were vital for successful colonial rule, spreading the English language and British values.[20] But while missionaries did often promote and support the imperial project, this could not be taken for granted. They were not the puppets of colonial governments, which they frequently defied. Their ministries did not always conveniently follow the official line. Porter elaborates this into a more fundamental argument about the nature of British imperialism. He rejects the notion that the forces behind imperial expansion were ever truly unified in either motives or objectives, that there ever was a single, monolithic imperial project. For Porter, 'a world in which the many different interests in overseas expansion were at cross purposes even when not largely detached from each other, often seems closer to reality'.[21] This perspective has made Porter one of the most fervent critics of recent attempts to postulate new unified theories of British imperialism.

Porter also vigorously rebuts the depiction of Christian missions as unremittingly racist and exploitative. Missionary thinking in the early nineteenth century tended to stress human equality, and as such was not inherently racist. This was demonstrated in the various Christian campaigns against the slave trade in the late eighteenth century, and slavery in the West Indies during the 1830s and 1840s.[22] Survival in often hostile environments forced missionaries to be sensitive of local cultures. Where possible they recruited local people to deliver the missionary message. Usually this discouraged high-handedness or indifference to the interests of the subject people.[23] Porter also stresses the benefits which missionaries brought to many of the less developed parts of the empire, in the form of schools, literacy, medicine and opportunities for social advancement for some of the poorest members of colonial societies.[24] Later in the nineteenth century, missionary theology also began to display greater interest and tolerance of non-Christian religions within the empire, as Christian scholarship began to reveal parallel ideas and beliefs in different religions. These trends tended to diminish or counteract tendencies within the missionary churches towards chauvinism or racism. Such developments were an integral aspect of the rugged independence of Christian missions from the imperial state.

Porter's arguments have been extensively developed in his book *Religion Versus Empire*, a major review of the relationship between Protestant missionaries and the British empire down to 1914.[25] Porter's scepticism about the notion that religion and missionary organisations were somehow integral to both the imperial project and the exploitation of subject peoples, is if anything, stated even more forcefully. Ultimately missionary Christianity fell under indigenous influences, and as frequently represented a force for liberation as it did for repression. Porter's model of missionary Christianity as a force which was interconnected with British imperial expansion, yet fiercely independent from the apparatus of the British imperial state, stands to be tested by further research.

Porter has also championed the need for imperial historians to address the wider role of humanitarian movements such as the Anti-Slavery movement and the Aborigine Protection Society in shaping imperial policy. In the imperial context, humanitarianism dictated that imperial power had to be justified by moral obligation to those under colonial rule. In effect, empire was an exercise in Trusteeship of the welfare of less civilised peoples, an idea which owed its origins to the Enlightenment of the eighteenth century. Porter contends that there were two contrasting and potentially conflicting motive forces behind imperial humanitarianism. Firstly, a conviction that there should be limits to how far imperial rule should interfere with local culture and customs, that respect for indigenous religions and values was an obligation of the conqueror; but secondly a belief that there was also a duty to educate and morally uplift – an interventionist prescription largely driven by evangelical Christianity. Porter argues that the activities of a plethora of humanitarian organisations in Britain and overseas constituted a restraining influence which helped curb the worst excesses of imperial rule such as slavery and the slave trade. But Porter readily acknowledges that humanitarian movement relations with British imperialism tended to be mutually reinforcing. On the one hand, humanitarians welcomed British imperial power and global reach in challenging the slave trade on the high seas and in the non-European world. On the other, carefully selected concessions to humanitarian causes by the Colonial Office or local colonial administrations provided useful evidence that empire was, after all, a civilising mission. In this sense humanitarianism never posed serious questions about the moral validity of British imperialism. Moreover, after the mid-nineteenth century, when notions of white superiority and negative stereotypes of other races gained intellectual respectability, humanitarian ambitions for the subject peoples were duly scaled down to conform with less egalitarian assessments of their potential for civilisation. As a result, the achievements of the humanitarians in the context of empire remained limited, though nonetheless significant in checking the more exploitative tendencies of British imperialism.[26]

A recent case study of the impact of missionary work in Jamaica during the nineteenth century offers many insights into the roles of religion and humanitarianism in empire. It examines not only the forces which shaped the missionary work in Jamaica itself, but also the ways in which opinion at the periphery and in the metropole interacted, producing dynamic changes in both over time. Catherine Hall's *Civilising Subjects* offers not only a very thorough exploration of how missionary behaviour was shaped at the periphery, but also of the shifting relationship between Britain and the colonies in the realm of ideas and perceptions of the empire.[27] Professor of Modern British Social and Cultural History at University College London, Hall (b. 1946) was drawn to the subject of her study, Jamaica, for deeply personal reasons. She is the daughter of a Northamptonshire Baptist minister, whose church enjoyed historic connections with the early Baptist missionaries to Jamaica. She married Stuart Hall, later the eminent Professor of Cultural Studies at the University of Birmingham and the Open University, and a Jamaican by origin. Catherine Hall studied and lived in Birmingham in the 1960s and 1970s, experiencing at first hand the British city which figures prominently in *Civilising Subjects*, and she visited Jamaica on a number of occasions. As a result, the book is strengthened by a pervading sense of personal as well as intellectual engagement with the subject.

Hall explores the missionary experience in two very different locations: in Jamaica and in Birmingham in Britain during the period 1830 to 1867. She examines the ideology and strategies of several generations of clerics who went to the island, tracing how these evolved during the period. During the 1820s and 30s the missionaries were in the vanguard of the resistance first to slavery, and later the system of indentured labour which the plantation owners tried to introduce. In this phase, the missionaries demonstrated the independent role outlined by Porter in his analysis of religion within the empire. Missionaries displayed great courage in resisting violent intimidation by the planters, and assiduously built up their black congregations. They asserted black equality and pressed for political reforms to strengthen the position of blacks in Jamaican society. At the same time however, the white missionary community worried that the existing black Baptist community was 'too culturally African, and sought to establish a distinct and separate identity.[28] White missionary acknowledgement that blacks were the potential equals of whites morally and intellectually, was qualified by the belief that this depended upon the eradication of the existing black culture, with all its African attributes, and its replacement by white European values, morality and standards of behaviour. In this respect, even at the height of their support for black rights, white missionaries still subscribed to a firm notion of white, Protestant cultural and moral supremacy.

But the championing of black racial equality by this earlier generation of white missionaries was gradually weakened and subverted by events. In the 1840s, economic depression and the severing of formal financial links with parent missionary societies severely undermined the Jamaican missionary churches. Even more worrying was the growing confidence of black members of the flock, who began to use their power within the churches to revive their own cultural traditions. White missionary leaders were deeply alarmed by the phenomenon of 'Myalism', a form of Christianity which incorporated elements of African religious tradition, including belief in the influence of the spirit world in daily affairs.[29] Increasingly white missionary leaders found themselves at odds with black Christian leaders eager to assert their own independent version of the faith. By the 1860s, when a new phase of religious revival on the island displayed an even greater

African influence, many white missionaries believed that their black charges were straying from the path chosen for them.[30] By then doubts were being expressed about the capacity of the 'excitable negro' to be assimilated fully into Christian civilisation. Hall reinforces Bernard Semmel's classic study of the Morant Bay uprising of 1865, when eighteen officials were killed by black rioters, showing how it helped consolidate the racist perspective which became increasingly prevalent in England during the later nineteenth century.[31]

Parallel to these developments, Hall also demonstrates a hardening of racist attitudes in Birmingham, where the anti-slavery activities in the 1830s of the city's leading nonconformist businessmen, gave way to much more negative, hierarchical and racist perceptions of humanity. Herein lay the basis for the rise of Joseph Chamberlain's triumphalist conception of empire, in which separate races would be treated very differently.[32] Throughout the book Hall traces missionary attitudes, values and social organisation, both in Jamaica and Britain. But what is particularly original in her approach is the attempt to explain how attitudes and politics in the metropole and on the periphery interacted with and shaped each other, in a dynamic and complex way. The majority of imperial case studies have tended to place most emphasis upon developments on the periphery, a legacy of the Gallagher and Robinson interpretation of British imperialism. In contrast, Hall shows there was a dialogue about Jamaica's black population between interested metropolitan and peripheral groups. This exchange of views shaped events and policies in both Jamaica and Britain, and gradually consolidated a much more negative perception of blacks at home and in the colony. It is an approach which has much to recommend it in explaining the origins of certain changes in cultural attitudes towards empire.

Of course, race and empire have long been connected by imperial historians, particularly those from former colonies in Africa, Asia or the West Indies, where attitudes of white racial superiority dominated, especially in the late Victorian period. It is widely accepted that the later nineteenth century witnessed a pronounced hardening of racial attitudes. Certainly there had always been a vocal strain of racist opinion in British intellectual life throughout the nineteenth century, as apparent in the pro-slavery writings of men such as Edward Long (1734–1813), and in Thomas Carlyle's (1795–1881) *Occasional Discourse on the Nigger Question* of 1853.[33] Ranged against these, however, were evangelical Christians who believed that all human beings were fundamentally in the eyes of God, even if some had progressed more quickly along the road to moral enlightenment and civilised material progress. Porter argues that in this sense the Christian missionary message was profoundly anti-racist, stressing a universal human potential for redemption and advancement.[34] From this conviction sprang the great late eighteenth-century campaign against the slave trade, and the successful agitation against slavery in the West Indies of the 1820s and 1830s. Hall shows that throughout the mid century there had been a passionate struggle between racist and anti-racist schools of thought, in which the latter more than held its own. From mid-century however, several developments swung the balance of the debate towards racism. The Indian rebellion of 1857 and its ferocity followed several decades of British reforming initiatives designed to induct Indians into the ways of the 'civilised' world, cast doubt on the capacity of Indians for enlightenment. The Morant Bay disorders reprised the trauma and anxiety of post 1857 India, and consolidated a growing conviction that Asians and Africans were impervious to civilising reform because of their racial characteristics. Charles Darwin's (1809–82) *The Origin of Species* also challenged the Christian view of the origins of humanity, and its emphasis upon natural selection as the motor force of the evolution of species, suggested to some that variations of colour and physiognomy between humans signalled more fundamental differences between them.[35] Even before these developments, a new literature was emerging which attempted to explain racial variety, with a strong undercurrent of white supremacism. Robert Knox's (1791–1862) *The Races of Men* was typical of this genre which celebrated supposed white superiority over other races.[36] It was also reflected in the writings of Froude, Seeley and others, who all stressed the natural, superior qualities of the Anglo-Saxon race which had allowed them to dominate the world.

Yet in spite of this consensus among historians about the emergence of racism as a defining feature of late Victorian imperialism, studies which are specifically dedicated to the phenomenon of racism in the British empire are surprisingly thin on the ground. Kiernan's *The Lords of Human Kind* certainly takes race as a major theme, but it is concerned with wider issues of cultural perception as well.[37] Among the others, Christine Bolt's *Victorian Attitudes to Race* and Douglas Lorimer's *Colour Class and the Victorians* remain the most influential works.[38] Bolt (b. 1940), now Emeritus Professor of History at the University of Kent, Canterbury, and a renowned writer on American slavery, feminist history as well as race, made several claims about the nature of British attitudes to subject peoples of different colour. She argued that a hierarchy of races existed in the British mind, in which white Anglo-Saxons formed the upper layer, beneath which came the Indians, whose 'inferior' colour was marginally mitigated by their common 'Aryan' ancestry with Europeans, their sophisticated cultural history and the wealth and high social status enjoyed by their leaders. At the bottom was the African black, whose poverty, former slave status, together with his supposed absence of history and culture, offended white British sensibilities of class as well as race.[39] For Bolt, skin colour was the defining element in racial distinction, and the darker the skin the more pronounced the degree of inferiority, and undesirability of interbreeding.[40]

Bolt's work was complemented by Lorimer's *Colour, Class and the Victorians* and Paul Rich's *Race and Empire in British Politics*. Lorimer is a Canadian historian of nineteenth-century British society and racism, and Rich a political scientist at the University of Melbourne, whose subsequent work has focused mainly on South Africa in the twentieth century. Their perspectives of British society as outsiders in former white colonies lend their work an insightful quality. Lorimer argued that the tendency towards a more pessimistic, biologically determined view of human nature was at the heart of the new racism of the mid-Victorian period. He contended that the tendency to downplay the importance of individual distinctiveness and emphasise the dominance of inherited traits, informed the emergence of negative stereotypes of social class as well as race. Rich was also intrigued by the intensification of racist attitudes during the nineteenth century. He rejected Peter Fryer's earlier thesis that Victorian racism emerged from the activities of an influential planter class in Britain and the West Indies whose economic interest in black slavery led them to propagate racist attitudes throughout British society as the nineteenth century progressed.[41] Fryer, a former communist journalist and historian, whose left wing political perspective led him to relate the emergence of racism to capitalism, offers something of a standard Marxist interpretation of the phenomenon. But for Rich, the 'slave plantocracy' were always too isolated even in the eighteenth century, and Britain's black population too small, for these to be the main factors in the rise of racist ideology. In any case, the ascendancy of racism later in the nineteenth century post-dated the abolitions of first the slave and trade and then slavery in the West Indies by the 1830s.[42] The roots of late Victorian racism lay instead in the economic imperatives imposed by an expanding overseas empire which required a vast labour force to service and develop its economic potential. The characterisation of blacks and other non-white races as biologically inferior provided a convenient justification not only for stripping them of their land and sovereignty, but also for the ruthless methods used to make them work for their new masters. Only through the sternest coercion would the feckless black 'quashee' of Carlyle's imagination maximise the production of the land 'for the benefit of all mankind'.[43] Coupled with this, the late Victorian high point of imperialism encouraged notions of Anglo-Saxon superiority, as demonstrated by the astonishing technological leap forward made by the British industrial revolution, and the ease with which that race acquired so much of the world.[44]

Yet Rich concurs with numerous other historians in arguing that there were factors which restrained the development of racism. For him, British 'middle opinion' (the prevailing outlook of the educated middle classes) acted as a check on the development of a more rigorous and extreme racist ideology in Britain. In contrast with mainland Europe, the strength of British liberalism and its belief in the capacity for social improvement through reform, coupled with popular distrust of intellectuals and ideas, prevented the emergence of a dominant racist social theory.[45] Certainly this view receives considerable support from other historians. As shown, Porter and Hall both stress the activities and influence of religious ideology as a counter weight to racist attitudes in the nineteenth century, although the latter did make considerable headway in the later Victorian period. Colley's emphasis upon the fragility of the British empire, and its dependence upon collaborators of different religion and ethnicity, also points to the mitigation of race as a defining factor in the imperial experience. For Cannadine, considerations of social status often figured more prominently than race in the British mind in dealings with locals at the periphery. Thus the practical demands of imperial governance constrained the development of racist ideology. As a result, although there is a consensus that British racial attitudes certainly hardened in the later nineteenth century, it is also widely held that these were never strong enough to permit the emergence of an extremist ideology bent on conquest solely on the grounds of the alleged biological inferiority of certain races. While this did not prevent sporadic episodes of racist atrocity and persecution within the empire, it did at least largely preclude the kind of planned and systematic genocide which became such a central feature of some of the new empires of the twentieth century, notably that of Nazi Germany. As such, racist argument was more a device to justify British conquests after the event, than a major driving force behind expansion.

The emergence of feminist ideology and writing since the 1970s has also influenced the study of the British empire. In the following decades, gender became a major new area of study for imperial historians, not least because it offered new insights into how the realms of imperial policy and the private lives of empire builders interacted and shaped each other. As Diane Wylie, Associate Professor of History at Boston University in the USA argues, no account of empire could ever be complete 'if half the population were omitted'.[46] A number of debates emerged surrounding the question of gender and empire. One of the earliest controversies concerned the effect on British imperial rule of the arrival at the periphery of large numbers of white women. In 1978, Lewis H. Gann (1925–97) and Peter Duignan, Senior Fellows at the Hoover Institution in the USA, lent academic credibility to the view, expressed by many male contemporary commentators, that the presence of women in the colonies served to undermine relations between British imperial officials and their 'native' subjects, by ending the practice of racial inter-marriage.[47]

Rebuttal of this interpretation has been comprehensive. Now Emeritus Reader in British Imperial History at the University of Cambridge, Ronald Hyam's extensive and controversial study of sexuality in the British empire rejected this scapegoating of white women in the empire, contending that they largely conformed to white male expectations, and even displayed greater empathy towards other races.[48] This more sympathetic view has been bolstered by various case studies of philanthropic and welfare development work by women in the empire.[49] In the case of Malaya, Janice Brownfoot even argues that white women working in education often used their influence to challenge British imperialist assumptions. They certainly did not act as though they were the mere purveyors of imperial culture to willing collaborators.[50] However, these studies also demonstrate that white women willingly and actively participated in the imperial project, even where they tried to mitigate its most pernicious effects. Wylie's conclusion, that on the whole white women were predominantly complicit in, rather resistant to imperial rule, is difficult to reject.[51]

Another interesting perspective has concentrated upon the patterns of day-to-day life of white women in the empire, and how this affected inter-racial and class relationships. In the case of India, several historians have linked white male sexual jealousy of white women as a factor which promoted racist attitudes.[52] Indrani Sen, lecturer in the English department at the University of Delhi, in particular has produced an intricate analysis, which demonstrates how class, gender and racial attitudes came to be mutually reinforcing within the context of empire.[53] She argues that the empire served to harden not only racial and class barriers, but also negative perceptions of women as weaker or inferior beings.[54] Indeed, some contemporaries even drew comparisons between women and the 'lower races' in terms of their inferiority to the white male. Excessive emotionality, limited rationality and childlike qualities were frequently attributed to both white women and the non-white races, implying the need for patriarchal white mastery over both. Sen quotes the phrenologist Carl Vogt's definitive statement of 1864: 'The skulls of man and woman are to be separated as if they belonged to two different species ... we may therefore say that the type of the female skull approaches, in many respects, that of the infant, and in a still greater degree, that of the lower races.'[55]

Thus both natives and white women required the firm hand of white male governance. There was particular anxiety about the effects of exposing 'pure' white women to the supposedly uncontrolled sexuality of Indian culture, and also about exciting the rumoured passions of Indian males for white female flesh. Sen argues that in this respect, the presence of white women in India served to heighten white male prejudices and fears about both Indian men and white women, specifically that left unchecked the latter would fall prey to the lustful advances of the former. In this way in the colonies, the white male's racism and sexism fed off and reinforced each other.

White male fears about the vulnerability of the memsahib to her own and native male passions, led to her effective social isolation. 'Respectable' white women in India enjoyed high social status, domestic dominance over an army of Indian servants and a high material standard of living, but at the heavy price of limited social intercourse and blighted opportunities for personal development. Indeed, this remoteness from native society became a badge of class distinction within the white community. Sen describes it as a kind of 'purdah'.[56] Although all white women were regarded as belonging to the ruling elite, some enjoyed higher status than others, and one expression of this was the segregation of white women to the point where the only Indian males they came into contact with were servants. Those white women who embraced contact with Indians such as missionaries, were regarded as socially inferior, and frequently ostracised by white society.[57] But the price paid by high status white women was very high indeed. Sen notes the high incidence of depression and mental illness among the memsahibs, a trend which was aggravated by the practice of sending their children home to be educated. Not only were female missionaries spared such extreme social isolation, they also enjoyed greater opportunities to influence imperial development through their religious and educational activities.[58] What Sen offers, therefore, is a complex picture of a stratified white female society in India, within which status was determined by interlocking notions of gender roles, race and social class.

The position of white women within empire has inevitably attracted the interest of post-colonial theory. Drawing upon literary evidence and psychoanalytical theory, Anne McClintock, Simone de Beauvoir Professor of English and Gender Studies at the University of Wisconsin, USA, tries to explore the various identities created for women within the imperial context.[59] Like Sen, she is particularly interested in how race, class and gender interacted with each other to shape female perceptions of themselves. While McClintock's work is diligently researched, like much post-colonial theory it has been criticised for its rejection of mainstream historical method.[60] McClintock's refusal to be constrained by the 'sanctioned binaries-coloniser-colonised, self-other, dominance-resistance, metropolis-colony, colonial-post-colonial', leads her to eschew the contextualisation of her work within imperial political developments.[61] As a result, her work has a disjointed and anecdotal quality which makes it difficult for the reader to relate her work to wider historical developments. Consequently, all too frequently, her arguments are unclear.

The impact of British imperialism on 'native' women has been another area for debate. A variety of historical accounts argue that indigenous women in several colonies suffered oppression both before and after imperial conquest, as traditional methods of subordinating women were displaced by colonial legislation or new foreign capitalist forms of exploitation.[62] Post-colonial theory argues that empire effectively silenced native women, especially in India, by imposing upon them the lowest possible status and the most limited opportunities. But this is to ignore some of the positive effects of British rule. Brownfoot's study of Malaya has already been mentioned, and it is difficult to argue that British efforts to outlaw Sati and infanticide in India, or female circumcision in east Africa, were anything other than major improvements in the lives of indigenous women. Certainly recent studies demonstrate how native women were incorporated into the economic structures of colonialism. The use of local female labour in factories and mines was well established in parts of India and Africa, as Rosalind O'Hanlon demonstrates, and this had profound effects upon traditional indigenous societies.[63] Much detailed research into the position of both white and indigenous women under British imperial rule continues, and the debates about the extent to which the former were victims or accomplices, and the latter victims or beneficiaries, will constitute an important field of future historical writing. Gender is now almost as firmly established as a tool of analysis as race or class.

Of course, social class and national identity have also been key areas of interest for analysts of the British empire. As seen, Hobson identified various social groups who benefited directly from empire, and who were therefore its keenest supporters. The financiers of the City of London were particularly singled out by him as an aggressive sector of British society who pushed the bounds of empire forward. As will be seen in the next chapter, Cain and Hopkins also pinpoint this group, together with their allies within the landed elite, as key drivers of imperial expansion. Other historians have identified manufacturers and merchants hungry for overseas markets or supplies of produce, as significant promoters of empire. Mackenzie, Colley and Bayly have recognised British imperialism as a factor which in the eighteenth century helped cement a discrete British identity, particularly within the middle classes and ruling elites.[64] Perhaps the keenest interest however, has been shown in the question of class and empire in the Victorian period. The reasons for this are not difficult to identify. British society had undergone a dramatic period of upheaval, involving the emergence of several new classes associated with industry: the capitalists, blue-collar workers and later in the century white-collar employees. Out of these economic and social changes emerged a new mass culture, in which an increasingly literate and educated population could participate. There was a new political climate, exemplified by the growth of class-based pressure groups competing for influence in a political system which was moving, through a series of enfranchising Reform Acts, towards mass democracy. Significantly the last twenty years of the nineteenth century saw the growth of a mass working-class movement in the form of the trade unions, culminating ultimately in the formation of the Labour Party in 1903. Though its philosophy was vague, it aspired to a socialist vision of an equal society in which wealth and ownership of the means of production would be more evenly distributed. Combined with emerging notions of political equality within a mass parliamentary democracy, this amounted to something a radical shift to the left in British political culture. Yet it coincided not with a weakening of British imperialism and its culture of racial inequality, economic exploitation and militarism, but with its elevation to new heights. Paradoxically, domestic radicalism and desire for reform co-existed with enthusiasm for sabre-rattling, conquest and the subordination of 'lesser' peoples. Since the mid-1980s, this has been the focus of much of the work of John Mackenzie (b. 1943), formerly Professor of Imperial History at the University of Lancaster, and now associated with the Research Institute for Irish and Scottish Studies at the University of Aberdeen.[65]

John Mackenzie has been one of the leading historians of class, culture and empire since the early 1980s. Originally interested in the history of African migrations in the 1960s, Mackenzie's interest in the use of the then unconventional techniques of oral history, and a growing conviction that imperial history was too dominated by the study of the white British elite and abstract economic forces, led him to the view that the subject needed to be widened in both approach and the range of sources used. In particular, Mackenzie was struck by the tendency of many historians to separately compartmentalise British domestic and British imperial history, inferring that empire was only of limited significance to the mass of the British population. In spite of opposition to his ideas in certain elevated quarters, Mackenzie pioneered the use of a wide range of new sources previously untapped in relation to the emergence of popular imperialism – contemporary popular literature, drama, comics and similar depositories of popular culture. Mackenzie freely concedes that in this he was fortunate in catching a tide which swept along a new generation of scholars. But he quickly established himself as a leading figure in this new movement. He was instrumental in the establishment of the Manchester University Press series *Studies in Imperialism*, which pioneered and helped to establish a rich literature on the cultural and social aspects of British imperialism, especially in areas such as popular culture, race, sexuality and feminism. To date over fifty books have been published in the series, and it is no exaggeration to say that it has transformed and hugely enriched the general literature on British imperialism. Latterly, Mackenzie has moved into the area of imperialism and the natural world, and his status as a historian of imperial culture lent weight to his forthright criticism of Said's *Orientalism* referred to in the previous chapter, in spite of inciting the fury of supporters of post-colonial theory.[66]

Mackenzie identifies the growth of an imperial culture in Britain from the late eighteenth century which promoted a strong sense of national identity. This cut across both class and ethnic boundaries. It reached a very large audience, even in the early nineteenth century, through a wide variety of media. The paintings of famous imperial figures and battles in the eighteenth century, especially in an Indian setting, conveyed both a sense of what the orient was like, and an awareness of the need for British unity in the face of rival empires, both European and eastern.[67] The popular theatre took imperial themes to a wider public, establishing a strong affinity empire among the mass of the British people even before the age of 'New Imperialism'. Mackenzie rejects Max Beloff's argument that the British 'were not an imperially minded people'.[68] Even before the establishment of modern mass culture, there was already a strong identification with empire among a large section of the British population.

Mackenzie argues that the late Victorian period saw the consolidation of this pro-imperial sentiment into a powerful popular culture. It welded together British society in a way that entrenched the power of conservative political and social forces, in spite of the rise of radical, working class, democratic organisations. There emerged an 'ideological cluster', a series of interlocking beliefs, values and ideas, which together helped instil a general sense of loyalty to Britain and its empire, regardless of the emergence of working class solidarity or other challenges to the social and political establishment. These included racial stereotyping, the idealisation of the Anglo-Saxon peoples, a devotion to royalty and other symbols of the traditional social order, the popular celebration of imperial heroes such as General Gordon, and the idealisation of the army and other branches of the military service. Organised religion, with its history of missionary endeavour to improve the lot of the lower races of the empire, also provided a moral and mystical justification for empire.[69] Mackenzie notes that some of the public institutions which benefited from the new imperial culture, such as the armed services and even the Crown, had previously suffered low popular esteem. Imperialism transformed their standing in public opinion.[70] Much of the transmission of this new culture was through skilful use of propaganda by the state and supporters of the imperial ideal. The music hall, popular music, popular literature, the newspapers, advertising, public ceremonies, the pulpit, sport, the school classroom, youth movements, toys and other forms of childhood recreation were all deployed to capture public affection for empire across the social spectrum. In the early twentieth century, cinema and radio were added to the armoury of mass media at the disposal of the promoters of British imperialism. Mackenzie argues that all of this worked. It created a mass popular support for empire which at times was almost tangible. This was never more evident than in the public celebrations following the relief of Mafeking during the Boer War. It bound together the social classes and the various ethnic groups who made up the British Isles in a profound sense of nationhood and collective racial superiority. Imperial idealists such as Joseph Chamberlain even wanted to extend this collective identity to the white Anglo-Saxons of the dominions, in the ambitious project of transcontinental imperial state building which was the Tariff Reform campaign.

In support of Mackenzie, a series of specialist studies fleshed out his thesis of the mass transmission of imperialist values. The most important of these was probably *Imperialism and Popular Culture*, a volume of essays edited by Mackenzie himself and published in 1986.[71] One of these, by Penny Summerfield, expanded upon her earlier argument (taken up by Mackenzie) that the music hall became a vehicle for imperialist propaganda.[72] Summerfield charted the increasing bellicosity of songs, sketches and other aspects of the genre as the end of the nineteenth century approached. She detected a decline in depictions of empire as morally uplifting, with ever greater emphasis upon British power for its own sake. Crucially, she argued that the potency of the medium lay in the social diversity of music hall audiences, which included members of the respectable middle class as well as the workers.[73] John Springhall constructed a similar argument for the role of popular art in the promotion of empire, particularly in the portrayal of heroic deeds by famous

British soldiers. He contended that many of the paintings of the period helped transform the previously poor reputation of the British army into one of popular pride by the last decades of the nineteenth century.[74] Bratton's review of children's popular fiction during the Victorian and Edwardian periods showed how pro-imperialist sentiments were inculcated from a very early age.[75]

Some of this work has also focused upon the developing culture of those who manned the imperial machine, who filled the ranks of the military and colonial services which ran empire at the sharp end. The Oxford expert in West African history, Anthony Kirk-Greene, produced a comprehensive study of the British imperial service which explores the backgrounds and formative influences which shaped imperial administrators from the mid-nineteenth century onwards.[76] He notes in particular the importance of the personal qualities which the public schools instilled in the sons of the upper middle classes, which particularly fitted them for imperial service. The ability to cope with loneliness and physical hardship, athleticism, emotional restraint and a shared Christian moral code were all attributes which fitted young men for the rigours of the colonial world.[77] Professor J.A. Mangan, Director of the International Centre for Sport, Socialisation and Society at De Montfort University, also emphasises the importance of the public schools, particularly their emphasis upon games and the development of leadership skills, in the conscious preparation of boys for imperial careers.[78] As will be seen in the next chapter, Cain and Hopkins also focus upon the public schools as the seedbed of the imperial elite, though their definition of it extends beyond the narrow confines of the imperial bureaucracy.

This and the previous chapter provide some insight into the late twentieth-century explosion of interest in the varied aspects of British culture which shaped and were shaped by imperialism. It is a fascination which shows little sign of waning, as demonstrated by the continuing stream of publications in this field. Ultimately however, there is a central question which must be asked: to what extent were such cultural factors as racial or religious prejudice, missionary zeal or an emergent sense of British identity actually responsible for the rise of the British empire? It has to be conceded that the evidence in support of cultural factors as the main driving force behind British imperialism is at best, patchy. Running counter to Said's assertion of an orientalist ideology which predisposed western Christian powers towards imperial conquest, is the tradition within Christianity and western culture which not only stressed human universalism and actively resisted slavery, but also promoted education and notions of equality among the conquered peoples. Although late Victorian culture became increasingly racist, sexist and snobbish, there were contrary trends which necessitated the incorporation of members of 'lesser' races, women and even the lower orders of the white race into the imperial project, as Cannadine, O'Hanlon and Colley all show. It is hard to attribute any single episode of British conquest solely or even predominantly to a sense of racial or cultural superiority, though such beliefs certainly contributed to those outcomes. In this respect, cultural factors tended to be climatic in their role, shaping assumptions and attitudes in ways which made imperialist aggression more likely, rather than constituting the principal reason for conquest. Once a region was subsumed into the empire however, the nature and effects of British governance were profoundly shaped by cultural influences, as most of the works cited amply demonstrate. In conclusion, cultural influences tended to be most important in determining the form and effects of British rule, and in shaping British society itself, rather than in driving the imperial frontier forward.

Notes

1 See chapter 3, pp. 45–6.
2 See chapter 4, p. 78.
3 See, for example, J. F. Ade Ajayi, *Christian Missions in Nigeria 1841–1891: The Making of a New Elite* (London, 1965); E. A. Ayandele, *The Missionary Impact on Modern Nigeria, 1842–1914: A Political and Social Analysis* (London, 1965).
4 N. Etherington, 'Missions and empire', in R. W. Winks (ed.), *The Oxford History of the British Empire Volume 5: Historiography* (Oxford, 1999), pp. 303–14; p. 303.
5 A. Porter, 'Religion, missionary enthusiasm and empire', in A. Porter (ed.) *The Oxford History of the British Empire Volume 3: The Nineteenth Century* (Oxford, 1999), pp. 222–46; pp. 227–8.
6 See, for example, R. Gray, *Black Christians and White Missionaries* (New Haven, 1990).

7 H. Grafe, *The History of Christianity in Tamilnadu from 1800 to 1975* (Bangalore, 1990), p. 80.

8 Etherington, 'Missions and empire', p. 311; see also C. W. Forman, *The Island Churches of the South Pacific: Emergence in the Twentieth Century* (MaryKnoll, NY, 1982).

9 A. Porter, 'Religion, missionary enthusiasm and empire'; and idem, 'Religion and empire: British expansion in the long nineteenth century, 1780–1914', *Journal of Imperial and Commonwealth History* 20:3 (1993), 370–90.

10 Porter, 'Religion and empire', 375.

11 *Ibid.*

12 *Ibid.*, 378.

13 *Ibid.*, 386.

14 *Ibid.*, 371–2.

15 Porter, 'Religion, missionary enthusiasm and empire', 240.

16 Porter, 'Religion and empire', 377.

17 *Ibid.*, 381.

18 *Ibid.*, 373.

19 *Ibid.*, 381.

20 *Ibid.*, 372.

21 *Ibid.*, 376.

22 Porter, 'Religion, missionary enthusiasm and empire' p. 229.

23 *Ibid.*, pp. 238–9.

24 *Ibid.*, pp. 239–40.

25 A. Porter, *Religion Versus Empire: British Protestant Missionaries and Overseas Expansion, 1700–1914* (Manchester, 2004).

26 A. Porter, 'Trusteeship, anti-slavery and humanitarianism', in A. Porter (ed.), *The Oxford History of the British Empire Volume 3: The Nineteenth Century* (Oxford, 1991), pp. 198–21.

27 C. Hall, *Civilising Subjects: Metropole and Colony in the English Imagination 1830–1867* (Cambridge, 2002).

28 *Ibid.*, pp. 105–6.

29 *Ibid.*, pp. 151–2.

30 *Ibid.*, pp. 241–2.

31 B. Semmel, *The Governor Eyre Controversy* (London 1962).

32 *Ibid.*, pp. 432–3.

33 T. Carlyle, *Occasional Discourse on the Nigger Question* (London, 1853).

34 Porter, 'Religion, missionary enthusiasm and empire, p. 229.

35 C. Darwin, *On the Origin of Species by Means of Natural Selection* (London, 1859).

36 R. Knox, *The Races of Men* (London 1850–62, fragmentary).

37 V. Kiernan, *The Lords of Human Kind: Black Man, Yellow Man and White Man in the Age of Empire* (New York, 1969).

38 C. Bolt, *Victorian Attitudes to Race* (London, 1971); D.A. Lorimer, *Colour, Class and the Victorians: English Attitudes to the Negro in the Mid-Nineteenth Century* (Leicester, 1978).

39 *Ibid.*, pp. 208–11.

40 *Ibid.*, p. 214.

41 P. Fryer, *Staying Power: The History of Black People in Britain* (London, 1984).

42 P. Rich, *Race and Empire in British Politics* (Cambridge, 1986), p. 5.

43 *Ibid.*, p. 12.

44 *Ibid.*, pp. 13–16.

45 *Ibid.*, pp. 3–4.

46 D. Wylie, 'Disease, diet and gender: late twentieth-century perspectives on empire', in R. W. Winks (ed.), *The Oxford History of the British Empire: Volume V Historiography* (Oxford, 1999), pp. 277–89; p. 284.

47 L. H. Gann and P. Duignan, *The Rulers of British Africa 1870–1914* (London, 1978), pp. 141–57.

48 R. Hyam, *Empire and Sexuality: The British Experience* (Manchester, 1990), pp. 207–8.

49 C. Knapman, *White Women in Fiji, 1835–1930: The Ruin of Empire?* (London, 1986).

50 J. N. Brownfoot, 'Sisters under the skin: imperialism and the emancipation of women in Malaya, c. 1891–1941', in J. A. Mangan (ed.), *Making Imperial Mentalities: Socialisation and British Imperialism* (Manchester, 1990), pp. 46–73, p. 66.

51 Wylie, 'Disease, diet and gender', p. 286.

52 See, for example, K. Ballhatchet, *Race, Sex and Class under the Raj: Imperial Attitudes and Their Critics 1793–1905* (London, 1980).

53 I. Sen, 'Between power and "purdah": the white woman in British India, 1858–1900' *The Indian Economic and Social History Review* 34:3 (1997), 355–76.

54 *Ibid.*, 356.

55 *Ibid.*, 357.

56 *Ibid.*, 368.

57 *Ibid.*, 361.

58 *Ibid.*, 374.

59 A. McClintock, *Imperial Leather: Race, Gender and Sexuality in the Colonial Context* (London, 1995).

60 Wylie, 'Disease, diet and gender', p. 288.

61 McClintock, *Imperial Leather*, p. 15.

62 C. Robertson and I. Berger (eds), *Women and Class in Africa* (New York, 1986); E. Schmidt, *Peasants, Traders and Wives: Shona Women in the History of Zimbabwe 1870–1939* (London, 1992).

63 R. O'Hanlon, 'Gender in the British empire', in J. Brown and W. Roger Louis (eds), *The Oxford History of the British Empire Vol 4: The Twentieth century* (Oxford, 1999), pp. 379–97.

64 L. Colley, *Britons*; C. A. Bayly, *Imperial Meridien*; J. M. Mackenzie, 'Empire and metropolitan cultures', in A. Porter (ed.) *The Oxford History of the British Empire Vol 3: The Nineteenth Century*, pp. 270–93, pp. 273–4.

65 See particularly J. M. Mackenzie, *Propaganda and Empire: The Manipulation of British Public Opinion 1880–1960* (Manchester, 1984).

66 I am extremely grateful to Professor Mackenzie for kindly allowing me to read a copy of his paper given to a postgraduate seminar at the University of Melbourne on 1 July 2004, 'Methodologies and theoretical problems', which provided invaluable insights into the development of his ideas.

67 Mackenzie, 'Empire and metropolitan cultures', pp. 274–5.

68 *Ibid.*, p. 270; M. Beloff, *Britain's Liberal Empire Vol 1* (London, 1969) p. 19.
69 Mackenzie, *Propaganda and Empire* p. 2.
70 *Ibid.*, pp. 4–5.
71 J. M. Mackenzie (ed.), *Imperialism and Popular Culture* (Manchester, 1986).
72 P. Summerfield, 'Patriotism and empire: music hall entertainment, 1870–1914', in *ibid.*, pp. 17–48.
73 *Ibid.*, p. 42.
74 J. Springhall, '"Up guards and at them!" British imperialism and popular art', in *ibid.*, pp. 49–72.
75 J. S. Bratton, 'Of England, home and duty: the image of England in Victorian and Edwardian juvenile fiction', in *ibid.*, pp. 73–93.
76 A. Kirk-Greene, *Britain's Imperial Administrators 1858–1966* (Basingstoke, 2000).
77 *Ibid.*, pp. 8–19.
78 J. A. Mangan, *The Games Ethic and Imperialism: Aspects of the Diffusion of an Ideal* (Harmondsworth, 1986).

7

The metropole strikes back: the new debate about gentlemanly capitalism and empire, 1980–2004

The publication of the two volume *British Imperialism* by Peter Cain and Anthony Hopkins in 1993 sparked off a new debate about the British empire which continues to this day.[1] The pages of such prestigious journals as *Past and Present, The Historical Journal, the Journal of Imperial and Commonwealth History* and others have since been filled by articles debating the strengths and weaknesses of the Cain and Hopkins interpretation. At least two volumes of essays debating the thesis have appeared, drawing upon a global field of scholars, and in 2001 a revised, single-volume version of *British Imperialism* was published, responding to some of its early critics.[2] The Cain and Hopkins thesis did not only attract the interest of scholars of imperialism. Those concerned with questions about Britain's economic and social development were also drawn into the debate. The celebrated journalist Will Hutton drew heavily upon Cain and Hopkins in his influential analysis of Britain at the end of the twentieth century, *The State We're In*.[3] Several decades after the British empire dissolved, the debate about its origins has never been livelier, as a consequence of this new contribution.

In fact, while the books of 1993 brought their work to the centre of attention, Cain and Hopkins had already fleshed out their ideas in a series of lengthy and influential articles in the *Economic History Review*, the first of which appeared in 1980.[4] They had been working on their project since the early 1970s, when their collaboration at the University of Birmingham began. Hopkins (b. 1938), now Walter Prescott Webb Professor of History at the University of Texas in Austin, was building an international reputation for his work on the economic history of West Africa, while Cain, now Professor of History at Sheffield Hallam, was teaching a range of courses in the department of economic history.[5] They collaborated in the teaching of British economic expansion overseas, and this was instrumental in the development of their partnership. The University of Birmingham was in many ways a fitting backdrop for the development of a new interpretation of British imperialism. Founded in 1900, at the height of British imperial pomp, the University is dominated by the Joseph Chamberlain tower, a distinctive landmark on the Birmingham skyline, commemorating the career of Birmingham's most famous politician and probably Britain's foremost exponent of empire. Birmingham itself, of course, had been at the heart of the industrial revolution, and had long possessed a fierce self-confidence and optimism which symbolised national self-assurance during the age of empire. Civic expression of this has been something of a tradition in Birmingham; from the urban recon-struction of Chamberlain's day in the late nineteenth century, through the reinvention of the city as a shopper's paradise with the building of the Bull Ring in the 1960s, to the modern urban regeneration of the 1990s around the theme of Birmingham as a modern 'post-industrial Venice'. Cain and Hopkins' work, however, coincided with an unusual period of crisis and pessimism, as the malaise which befell British industry during the 1970s and 1980s hit Birmingham especially hard. The national crisis of industrial decline during this period contributed to a spirit of reassessment of British economic history, which is certainly reflected in the work of Cain and Hopkins on empire. It will be seen that their theory of imperial expansion was based upon a particular view of the nature of the British economy in the Victorian period, within which industry played a much more limited role than previously assumed. It is hard not to surmise that this was at least partly shaped by a contemporary local context of closing factories and urban decay.

It is important to understand that contemporary trends and research into British economic history, themselves influenced by the collapse of British industry, were also formative in the devel-opment of the Cain and Hopkins thesis. It is fair to say that British economic history underwent something of a revolution during the 1970s and 1980s. British 'de-industrialisation' in the 1970s, characterised by widespread bankruptcies, closures, and the disappearance of whole industries in the face of Japanese, German and other competition, prompted some historians to question the extent to which industry had ever been as influential in British economic and political development as had once been supposed. Historians such as Martin Wiener argued that Britain had long suffered from an aristocratic, 'anti-industrial' culture, which regarded industrial urbanisation as much of a blight on the landscape as the Gradgrindian factory capitalists and anarchic working class were on society.[6] While W. D. Rubinstein disagreed fundamentally with Wiener's notion of an anti-industrial British culture, his own work indicated that the importance of industry as a generator of fortunes and national wealth had been greatly exaggerated.[7] His research into the economic origins of the fortunes of the wealthiest people in Britain in the late nineteenth century showed that manufacturing accounted for only about a half of these, and actually declined slightly in the early twentieth century.[8] Land, commerce and finance together were much more important than industry in generating large personal and family fortunes. The significance of industry in British economic development was challenged further by the work of Professor Nicholas Crafts, which indicated that British industrial growth during the nineteenth century had been much slower than suggested by advocates of the theory of industrial 'revolution' such as Rostow.[9] At the same time, new work on the British economy suggested that the financial services sector of the economy had long played a much more central role in British economic prosperity than had previously been thought. The work of such historians as Clive Lee, P. K. O'Brien and Caglar Keyder transformed the perceptions of British economic historians, not least Cain and Hopkins.[10] Again, there were powerful contemporary resonances. As industry struggled in the 1980s, and former midlands boom towns like Birmingham became accustomed to the unfamiliar experience of mass unemployment and depression, the financial sector of the City of London went from strength to strength, as the 'big bang' of financial deregulation in the mid 1980s ushered in the new age of the fabulously rich City 'yuppie'.

The Cain and Hopkins thesis is probably the most ambitious

attempt yet to explain British imperialism. Its chronological scope is greater than any previous thesis attempting to explain the origins of the empire, tracing its rise from the late seventeenth century, to its demise in the last years of the twentieth. It not only links a complex theory of British economic, social and political development during the period to the wider phenomenon of imperial expansion, it also offers a series of geographical case studies, including India, Africa, the white dominions, Latin America, China and the middle east. The only substantial region to escape their scrutiny is south east Asia, and even this region has been incorporated into the thesis by another historian.[11] Its length, scope and sheer erudition are unmatched in the field, and their analysis of the nature of the British economy and society commands the attention of scholars concerned with modern British history in general. Crucially, Cain and Hopkins reassert the view held by earlier theorists of empire such as Hobson and Lenin, that the origins of British imperialism lay principally in the economic development of the metropole. They do not deny the importance of developments on the periphery as emphasised by Gallagher and Robinson, especially their capacity to determine the form that imperial dominance took. They assert, however, that the rise of the British empire cannot be fully understood as mere response to circumstances and events at the edge of empire, a stumbling into world dominance through absent-minded reactions to disorder at the frontier or the machinations of missionaries, merchants, colonial officials, or other self-interested 'men on the spot'. There were economic interests within British society which drove imperial expansion forward, and which enjoyed considerable leverage within the political structures of the British state. To explain fully who these groups were, and how they rose to a position of such power, Cain and Hopkins offer a new interpretation of the development of British society over the last three hundred years.

Their starting point is the last decades of the seventeenth century. It had been a century of civil war and intermittent political crises in the monarchy, stemming largely from the unresolved religious conflict between Catholics and Protestants for the English throne which had been the legacy of Henry VIII's turbulent reign. By the 1680s the fragility of the Protestant ascendancy under James II prompted his usurpation and replacement by William of Orange and Mary, and the early eighteenth-century establishment of the German, Protestant Hanoverian dynasty. From the outset this was a monarchy under siege, from both supporters of the old Stuart dynasty, and from their sympathisers among the major Catholic European powers. The very act of removing James II had increased the power of parliament at the expense of the Crown, an uncomfortable reality for the new rulers in 1688 and the new dynasty after 1714. European rivalries in the Americas and Asia, also contributed to this continuing, acute sense of insecurity among the new rulers, which could only be eased by the assembly of formidable military power. The problem was how to pay for this without inflicting punitive levels of taxation on the British population, particularly the landed elite, whose continuing loyalty was essential for dynastic survival. The solution lay in the major restructuring of the financial centre of the City London in the 1690s. The decade saw the foundation of the Bank of England, the effective creation of the Gold Standard and the establishment of the National Debt, the means by which the British state could borrow funds by issuing bonds and other securities onto the market.[12] The City of London, which had been a major centre for merchants and monied men since the late middle ages, was able to furnish the state with credit on sufficiently generous terms for it to sustain a powerful military wing without pushing taxation up to levels which would undermine the Hanoverian regime's delicate standing in the affections of the people. Over the next two hundred years, the City went from strength to strength, with the development of brokerage in bills of exchange, merchant banking, insurance, the stock market and a host of other flourishing financial services. As City money men moved to the centre of the state's strategy for managing the public finances, so they were drawn into the inner circle of political power at the summit of the political system. This political elevation of the financiers was underpinned by their simultaneous acceptance into the social milieu of the landed elite, the aristocrats and landowners who formed the ruling class of the nation. The agricultural revolution generated an expanding market in mortgages, bringing landowners and financiers into more frequent contact with each other. The wealth of some City financiers also brought them into closer social contact with the aristocracy, through intermarriage and the purchase of land and titles by the most successful City families.[13] One effect of this was to imbue upwardly mobile City merchants and bankers with the social outlook and values of their aristocratic superiors, inclining them towards adopting the same leisurely and cultured lifestyles. Leading City merchants and bankers were 'gentlemanly capitalists', men of business who nonetheless aspired to the cultural value system of the aristocracy. Thus by the nineteenth century, leading City merchant banking families such as the Barings and the Rothschilds had secured for themselves landed estates and peerages, and had in effect been absorbed into the landed elite, in spite of their foreign and commercial origins. All this amounted to the emergence of an informal but potent alliance between City financiers and the landed elite, which delivered influence to the former at the highest levels of the British state.

Cain and Hopkins argue that this had profound consequences for eighteenth-century British policy in a variety of fields, but particularly for overseas trade and empire. Many City interests were deeply involved in commercial enterprise with America and Asia, particularly through the great monopoly corporations such as the East India Company. City merchant bankers were instrumental in financing a significant expansion of British overseas trade, particularly with the New World. As a consequence, British imperial policy was shaped to meet their needs. When overseas trade failed to grow sufficiently to adequately remunerate gentlemanly capitalists, the British state was prevailed upon to fight a string of colonial wars with the Spanish, French and Dutch.[14] In India and the far east the East India Company, a central institution in the City during the period, enjoyed both support for its legal monopoly of trade in the 1770s and 1780s, and financial assistance from the state when the costs of governing their newly acquired territories outstripped the revenues extracted from the Company's Indian empire. Cain and Hopkins also argue that the City contributed to the loss of the American colonies in the 1770s. Following a long period of growth in the value of overseas trade in the earlier half of the century, a downturn from the 1760s resulted in mounting disenchantment among those planters, landowners and merchants in Boston, Virginia and other colonies who had borrowed heavily from creditors in the City of London.[15] Herein lay the origins of the revolt against British rule which led to ignominious defeat for George III.

This defeat for British imperial policy in America and the alliance of landed and City interests which sponsored it, coincided with the aforementioned financial crisis for the East India Company in India, which was only rescued by the intervention of the British government. The rise of Napoleon's expansionist French empire in the 1790s severely exacerbated these problems. Yet by 1815 the British emerged from these difficulties to become the world's leading imperial power. The City's command of money was of course central in making victory in the Napoleonic Wars possible, and Cain and Hopkins argue that the conflict saw both the consolidation of the British empire, and its utilisation in the war effort. But they recognise that this was also a profound period of change in the political and economic order at home. In the last decades of the eighteenth century a new economic interest group had emerged in the British provinces, particularly in the north west of England. The rise of British manufacturing industry substantially altered the balance of forces within British society. The manufacturers amassed formidable wealth, while the urban growth which factory production stimulated gave rise to a large and volatile industrial working class. The latter proved to be particularly troublesome during the war years, when luddism and other expressions of industrial discontent seemed to threaten widespread disorder and even revolution. The manufacturers themselves also showed a concerted willingness to assert their power, particularly in the areas of parliamentary reform and policies on overseas trade. From the beginning to the middle of the nineteenth century the alliance between the landed elite and the City financiers was compelled to surrender major political and economic concessions to these emergent forces. 'Old Corruption', that blanket term for monopoly, privilege and dishonest practices which prevailed under the old aristocratic order, now had to give way to a new age of meritocracy. Parliamentary reform in 1832, the ending of the East India Company's monopolies of trade to India and then China in 1813 and 1833, and the establishment of a policy of international free trade in the 1840s, were all designed to accommodate the needs and demands of industrial Britain.[16]

But Cain and Hopkins reject the notion that the establishment of the Gladstonian economic orthodoxy of free trade, balanced budgets and the Gold Standard represented an exclusive success for British manufacturers at the expense of land and finance. They contend that the balance of political power remained firmly in favour of the City gentlemanly capitalists. Their fortunes were generally larger than those of the provincial manufacturers, and their advantages of social integration into aristocratic circles and geographical proximity to the source of political power (London), continued to give them a decisive edge over industrial interests in the formation of imperial and economic policy. The gentlemanly capitalists, particularly the fabulously wealthy merchant banking dynasties such as the Barings and the Rothschilds, enjoyed an access to the senior politicians and patrician aristocratic families who governed Britain which was simply not available to the self-made manufacturers of Manchester or Glasgow. Their interests were not ignored, but neither did they exercise a decisive weight in issues of national political economy or imperial policy. Indeed, the principal beneficiaries of the free trade, low tax, fiscally prudent economic regime of late Victorian Britain were not the manufacturers but the mercantile and financial gentlemanly capitalists of the City. Industrial growth and free trade brought a huge expansion of Britain's overseas commerce. The real winners of the late Victorian international commercial expansion were the merchant banks and discount houses of London who specialised in supplying credit to domestic and foreign merchants engaged in international trade through the acceptance and discount of bills of exchange, together with the insurance companies and other financial institutions which also oiled the wheels of trade. The growth of the global economy provided new opportunities for the City. British industrial and demographic growth brought escalating demands for imported raw materials and food which could only be met by the development of key geographical sectors of the world economy. The demand for the capital necessary to open mines, railroads and docks in America, Africa and Asia could only be satisfied by those very City financiers who benefited so much from the expansion of international trade described above. From 1850 the City of London, particularly the Stock

Exchange, became the engine for the development of the global economy. Direct lending and share investment (portfolio investment) channelled some £4,000 million overseas between 1850 and 1914, in the process opening up the world's productive resources and incorporating them into the international economy.[17]

Meanwhile new gentlemanly capitalists rose to prominence in both the City and in the centre of political power. Their outlook continued to be shared by the aristocratic families who still dominated British parliamentary political life up to the First World War. Both groups continued to intermarry. They sent their children to the same public schools, went to the same round of social events and, were members of the same gentlemen's clubs in the capital. The wealthiest merchant bankers enjoyed a lifestyle that was indistinguishable from their social superiors. The nature of City business allowed for generous amounts of leisure time as well as the means to purchase titles, lands and fund an opulent social life.[18] It is unsurprising that in this intimate social world aristocrats and financiers tended to think similarly about political matters, adopt the same values and generally support each other in matters of personal interest. This social bond was further strengthened by the heavy representation of families from both groups in the machinery of government among professional politicians and senior civil servants. The City also enjoyed privileged access to state policy formation through its own influential organisations, particularly the Bank of England, the board of which was dominated by the most senior financiers in the square mile. The importance of financial services in generating invisible earnings, financing the state in times of emergency and generally helping to maintain international confidence in Great Britain, ensured that the Treasury and successive Chancellors of the Exchequer placed City interests at a premium in the formation of economic policy. Cain and Hopkins stress that the Gold Standard, free trade, low taxation and the balanced budgets were all policies which suited the City probably even more than industry.[19] Moreover as the provincial economic hub of the south east of England, the City could rely on the support of a range of interest groups who were conscious of their dependence on the financial markets, from the Brighton pensioner living on modest dividends from portfolio investments, to the army of white-collar clerks, domestic servants and other retainers whose employment depended ultimately upon the buoyancy of the City. All in all, argue Cain and Hopkins, this was a formidable basis for political power.

Cain and Hopkins argue that much of the expansion of the British empire in the nineteenth century can be explained by the activities of the gentlemanly capitalists and their allies in the administrative machinery of state. Overseas investments in mines, plantations, docks, or even in the governments of other nations, were all vulnerable to the vagaries of war, disorder and unforeseen political events. In order to protect them, investors and financiers sometimes had to persuade senior British politicians and officials to use limited force ('gunboat diplomacy') or more draconian actions, including conquest and absorption into the empire. But the empire was much more than a mere agglomeration of colonies acquired as a result of problems on the imperial periphery. It was the by-product of an emergent global British economic system based on free trade and the international movement of capital, and controlled by City gentlemanly capitalists.[20] In this respect, empire was just one aspect of a much larger process of British economic expansion, which took informal influence and occasionally direct control to nearly all parts of the world. The role of the gentlemanly capitalists in developing this system was not confined to political influence in the metropole or the funnelling of investment into this international system. They also developed a worldwide network of companies, merchants and other contacts upon whom they could rely for intelligence and co-operation in the pursuit of their global interests.

Cain and Hopkins also assert that the gentlemanly capitalists shared the ruling establishment's aversion for imperial conquest, and the expense and risks which it usually involved. After all, City men were not only just as reluctant to pay higher taxes as everyone else; they became by the late nineteenth century the most stalwart supporters of Gladstonian economic orthodoxy. From this perspective they tended to resist the various attempts in the late Victorian and early Edwardian period to challenge these principles. Even Joseph Chamberlain's ambitious programme for imperial unity behind a common tariff barrier, launched under the banner of the Tariff Reform League in 1903, received a mainly hostile response in the City.[21] An important consequence of this 'like mindedness' with the political establishment on economic issues and imperial expansion, was that when the City did throw its weight behind formal intervention, governments tended to treat their claims very sympathetically, as in Egypt in 1882.[22]

More frequently however, gentlemanly capitalists like politicians and civil servants, preferred informal imperialism to conquest. It was cheaper and more predictable, and the City's role as international supplier of capital provided the means of ensuring the co-operation of many indigenous ruling elites. For China and much of Latin America, for example, the City of London became the principal source of funds for a vast array of government activities and programmes of economic development. As a result, the governments of many of these countries adopted economic policies which were congenial to the interests of the City of London, including fiscal prudence and free trade.[23] These in turn facilitated yet further penetrations into the local economy by British capitalists of all kinds; industrial, mercantile as well as financial. Gallagher and Robinson's notion of an 'official mind' which preferred informal to formal empire is thus embraced but amended by Cain and Hopkins. Gentlemanly capitalists not only shared but actively supported the principles behind it, and substantially strengthened adherence to them. Moreover, they were the leading beneficiaries and agents of informal empire, since their financial interests there were both a source of wealth and a means of asserting control. But whereas Gallagher and Robinson emphasise a tendency to convert informal control to direct rule after 1870 as the pace of European imperial rivalry hotted up, Cain and Hopkins argue that Britain's informal empire actually grew much faster after 1870 than before, as City investment in new parts of the world extended the grip of the gentlemanly capitalists over the economic policies of more countries. Formal empire also expanded, for the reasons which Gallagher and Robinson cited, but for Cain and Hopkins the extension of informal influence, led by gentlemanly capitalist finance, was far more important and significant. They contend that the buoyancy and success of the City continued well into the twentieth century, and lent the empire a sturdy durability which many contemporaries and historians were slow to recognise. Many have viewed the Edwardian period and the First World War as the beginning of British imperial decline, as foreign industrial competition and the ruinous costs of global conflict set the British on an inevitable path of retreat from international dominance. Cain and Hopkins refute this, claiming that Britain's formal and informal empires weathered the trials of the first half of the century remarkably well. Even after the Second World War, policy makers, encouraged by prominent gentlemanly capitalists, sought to engineer Britain's return to global prominence through a strategy of imperial consolidation. Central to this was the Sterling Area currency bloc, under which empire, Commonwealth and other countries pooled their earnings of dollars to finance and minimise dependence upon imports from America. Even though imperial regeneration ultimately failed, it was not really until the end of the 1950s that the demise of Britain's empire and great power pretensions was clear to the country's ruling elite. While this book is concerned mainly with the debate about the rise of the British empire rather than its fall, it is important to note that this emphasis upon the enduring strength of empire until the mid-twentieth century is an important and controversial contribution to the historiographies of the British empire and modern British economic history.

It was perhaps inevitable, given the breathtaking ambition and erudition of this interpretation, that it would generate a long, complex and contentious debate. Cain and Hopkins provided much more than just a review of developments in the metropole, complex and controversial enough as that aspect of their work proved. They also tackled numerous specific case studies on the periphery, including Latin America, China, India, Canada, Australia, New Zealand and the whole of Africa. Inevitably this provoked challenges not merely from historians of empire, but also from specialist scholars of specific geographical regions. Discussion has revolved around numerous issues, most of which remained unresolved. What were these, and what light do they throw upon the validity or otherwise of the gentlemanly capitalist thesis?

Two related criticisms which have been levelled at Cain and

Hopkins may be discounted as misrepresentative and unfair. Dane Kennedy, in an essay concerned with post-colonial theory, offers a stinging dismissal of their work as a rehash of 'that old war horse of imperial history, J. A. Hobson, with a pinch of Schumpeter thrown in for flavour'.[24] While Cain and Hopkins draw upon Hobson's work, especially in relation to the financial interests of the City, to characterise their work as a mere reprise of Hobson's is caricature masquerading as criticism. Their scrupulous examination of the rise and evolution of the City over several centuries, its values, institutions and the network of relationships with the political establishment are simply not covered in Hobson's work. Furthermore they reject Hobson's conspiratorial version of how financiers persuaded politicians to act in their interest. Instead, they stress the common attitudes, values, social and institutional connexions which led to close consensus between the political and gentlemanly capitalist elites. The second accusation levelled at them, particularly by Fieldhouse, is that their explanation is fundamentally reductionist and monocausal, that it tends to depict gentlemanly capitalism as almost the sole driving force behind imperial expansion, to the exclusion of all other factors.[25] This allegation is hard to sustain in the face of Cain and Hopkins' scrupulous review of the various case studies of imperial expansion. Other influences are in fact accorded due recognition. In China, for example, they accept that in the first half of the nineteenth century it was as a market for the export of British and Indian manufactures that the British imperial appetite was first whetted, particularly in respect of the wars of 1839 to 1842 and 1858 to 1860.[26] In respect of the annexation of the Boer republics following the Boer War of 1899–1903, London financiers were implicated in the developments which led to the war but they were not the main culprits. Others, particularly Rhodes, Jameson and others on the spot, together with Chamberlain and other politicians in London who were worried by the prospect of an independent wealthy Boer state drawing the Cape colony into a Dutch-dominated federation, were equally, if not more culpable for the bloody events which followed.[27] In respect of West Africa, Cain and Hopkins have specifically rejected accusations to the effect that they tried to 'shoehorn' the region into their thesis by exaggerating the role played by gentlemanly capitalists in precipitating expansion there. Instead they readily acknowledge the greater role played by other economic and political interests.[28] On the whole, to dismiss their thesis as excessively monocausal is to oversimplify and overlook its complexity, which affords room for a wide range of contributory factors in the expansion of empire.

A more telling criticism focuses upon the question of Cain and Hopkins' assessment of the importance of industry in British economic and political development, and relations between industrialists and the gentlemanly capitalists of the City. It is true that Cain and Hopkins regard the manufacturers as playing a very small part in promoting imperial expansion.[29] Furthermore, industrialists are depicted as outsiders, with little national political influence and few contacts with either the landed or gentlemanly capitalist elites in London. Martin Daunton (b. 1949), now Professor of Economic History at Cambridge, strongly challenged this assessment of the position of manufacturing.[30] He casts doubt on research by historians such as Rubinstein, which suggests that industrial wealth was modest compared to the fortunes generated by merchant banking and other City-based financial services.[31] Daunton was also deeply sceptical about the alleged limited political clout enjoyed by industrialists. More generally, he attacked what he saw as a 'misplaced determinism' and 'crude reductionism' in much contemporary historical writing about social class formation, and a tendency towards the categorisation of people into perceived social groups with rather fixed views, social relations and aspirations.[32] Contrary to this, Daunton argued that the individuals out of whom society is assembled are in reality far less predictable in their attitudes and allegiances. The alleged distance between City financiers and provincial industrialists is also a particular target. Daunton pointed out, for example, that much of British manufacturing industry in the nineteenth century was heavily dependent upon export markets, a factor which brought them into very close contact with certain sections of the City. Drawing particularly upon the extensive work on relations between London merchants and provincial manufacturers undertaken by S. D. Chapman, Daunton noted for example that from about 1860 many provincial manufacturers organised their exports through commission agents and other merchant firms based in London.[33] In Daunton's view, the relationship between industry and finance was one based on complementarity rather than distance. As a result, commercial and social intercourse between City men and industrialists was probably much more common than Cain and Hopkins suggest, and opened avenues of industrial political influence which remain largely unexplored. Rubinstein offered a robust rejoinder to Daunton's doubts about the relative wealth of financiers and industrialists. He reasserted that by the latter half of the nineteenth century it was finance, not industry which was the most dynamic sector of Britain's expanding economy, and as such the real centre of commercial political influence.[34]

More recent work on the relationships between industrialists and City financial interests does tend to support certain aspects of Daunton's argument. Bowen shows that even such a stalwart institution of gentlemanly capitalism as the East India Company developed extensive contacts with provincial industry in order to generate commodities for profitable export.[35] A new article on abortive efforts in the 1830s to set up a London-based central bank for India, suggests that City based interests did not always get their own way when confronted by opposition from the provinces.[36] Fierce opposition from the Glasgow East India and China Association, working with dissident elements in the provincial cities and London, thwarted efforts by a London-led consortium of East India merchants to set up a bank with large assets (£5 million) which would have dominated Indian economic life. Provincial opposition was based principally upon the fear that this was a thinly disguised attempt to re-establish London's dominance over the trade with the east, following the abolition of the East India Company's remaining monopoly of trade with China in 1833. Resistance from the provincial interests succeeded because of extremely effective organisation, which ensured strong representation of their views in London, and close collaboration with opponents to the scheme based in the City. So effective was the resistance to the initial scheme of 1836, that three subsequent bank projects in the early 1840s were also abandoned. What this suggests is a far more effective degree of political organisation in the provinces, and a far greater degree of co-operation between provincial industrialists and City merchants than the Cain and

Hopkins model postulates. Other recent work also demonstrates that commercial relations between provincial manufacturers and City East India merchants commenced very early in the century, as early as the 1820s.[37] Relations between industry and finance thus seem to have been better developed and more complex than Cain and Hopkins have suggested, at least in the early nineteenth century.

Evidence from the late Victorian period also demonstrates a measure of collusion. In 1884–85, as part of their efforts to persuade the British government to annex Upper Burma the London finance house of Wallace Brothers, which had substantial logging and mercantile interests in the country, mobilised support in Glasgow and Manchester, particularly through their links with the chambers of commerce in those cities.[38] The balance of influence in this instance however, was decidedly in the favour of the London firm, which carefully orchestrated the provincial campaign to persuade the British government to invade. Its links with Manchester and Glasgow interests had grown from complex financial and mercantile connexions, and these were turned to good advantage in the crisis of 1885. Several points seem to emerge from these recent contributions. Overall, it does seem clear that the City and provincial industry were not so remote from each other, that from time to time their commercial and political interests either coincided or conflicted, and that these occasions prompted quite complex transactions between them. Secondly, the provincial men do not appear to have been wanting in ability to organise and lobby effectively. It should be remembered that the first chambers of commerce emerged in the great provincial industrial cities, and that London did not acquire one until 1881. Glasgow and Liverpool organised their East India and China associations in 1829/30, several years before London followed suit in 1836, and they sustained a deputation in London for several years before the passage of the 1833 East India Company Charter Act.[39] Thirdly, the success of Glasgow and their allies in resisting City interests on the Indian bank question demonstrates that in the first half of the century at least, the gentlemanly capitalists did not always get their way. As the century progressed, and City interests became wealthier and more influential, it does seem that an ascendancy over provincial interests was more firmly established. Gentlemanly capitalist connexions across a range of provincial interests and cities enabled them to perform a co-ordinating role which delivered political power into their hands.

Another argument which challenges the gentlemanly capitalist thesis highlights the composition of the City of London itself. Several historians challenge what they see as Cain and Hopkins' depiction of the City as a coherent body of interests which co-operated in pursuit of common economic and political goals.[40] Daunton notes the ethnic diversity of the City, and the very high turnover of people who moved into and out of financial services in the nineteenth century. He also notes the emergence of distinctive groups of merchant financiers who specialised in trade with different regions of the world. Their rise reflected the development of the global economy as a source of raw materials and food for the advanced industrialised nations, and their relations with each other were minimal. As a result, the City experienced a constant whirl of organisational and structural change. This fluidity, argues Daunton, casts doubt upon Cain and Hopkins' portrayal of the City as a cogent source of political influence. Disunity over such issues as tariff reform and bimetallism call into question the effectiveness of gentlemanly capitalist influence. Howe's work on City attitudes to free trade tends to support Daunton's argument, at least for the first half of the nineteenth century.[41] He also contends that neither the emergence of free trade, nor the substantial changes in the City which were wrought by the great financial crisis of 1847–48, welded together the disparate interest and ethnic groups who made up London's financial sector.[42]

The implication is that disunity in London must have diluted gentlemanly capitalist influence. But two points may be made in response to this argument. Firstly, the City was not an egalitarian economic environment; some were wealthier and more powerful than others. For the gentlemanly capitalism thesis to be vindicated what mattered was whether the most wealthy and powerful financiers, the Rothschilds, Barings and their like, were reasonably unified in their approach to government. This seems to have been the case, and it is important to note that these leading families had enjoyed a prominent position since the Napoleonic wars.

Secondly, although the City was divided ethnically and along lines of commodity and regional interest, it did not automatically follow that they were necessarily always in conflict with each other. Separation of interest often tended to minimise grounds for conflict. Besides, the City did not have to await the establishment of the London Chamber of Commerce in 1881 to develop a collective voice. The Bank of England and informal networks had long enabled financiers to manage differences and rally a common political front at times of crisis. Notwithstanding these points, Cain and Hopkins' assessment of gentlemanly capitalist influence does seem to be on stronger ground for the second rather than the first half of the nineteenth century. The period before 1850 saw great turmoil in the City, with the ending of the East India Company monopolies and the financial crises of the 1820s and late 1840s. The latter in particular caused huge upheaval and wholesale changes in personnel in the mercantile and financial sector. Disunity in the 1830s and 1840s over the fate of the East India Company monopoly, and over the various schemes for an Anglo-Indian central bank, challenge the notion of a seamless continuity of gentlemanly capitalist influence from the eighteenth century to the even greater successes of late Victorian Britain. There is a case for the argument that provincial industrial interests achieved rather more during the early Victorian period than mere accommodation of their demands.

Other historians have cited the British political system itself as a factor which casts doubt on gentlemanly capitalist influence over the British state. Darwin's scepticism about the existence of an 'official mind of empire' in the face of the myriad of domestic and imperial pressures on government applies as much to Cain and Hopkins' gentlemanly capitalist thesis as it does to Gallagher and Robinson's. In Darwin's words, 'the rough conditions of a decentralised parliamentary imperial state were hardly favourable to the authority, or even coherence, of an official mind'.[43] The nature of the pressures on the British state also changed during the period in ways which undercut the influence of gentlemanly capitalists. Late Victorian Britain saw not only substantial extensions of the franchise, but also the emergence of a democratised political culture in which trade unions, pressure groups, the press and public opinion all began to exert greater leverage over government policy. E. H. H. Green makes the point that by the late nineteenth century these larger political forces must have shaped policy formation as much if not more than the intimate ministries of gentlemanly capitalists.[44] But the case of the conquest of Burma in 1885 suggests that some gentlemanly capitalists were equal to the political demands of an emergent mass democracy. The skilful exploitation by Wallace Brothers of their provincial connexions to mount a co-ordinated campaign of organised business interests in favour of the annexation of Upper Burma demonstrates that City financiers were alive to the emergent democratic pressures which dictated the priorities of government.[45] It adds further weight to the point that relations between gentlemanly capitalists and industrialists were probably much more complex and important to both than is suggested by Cain and Hopkins. In addition, the relationship between the City and those powerful shapers of public opinion, the Press, may also have enabled gentlemanly capitalists to adapt to mass democratic political culture. Hobson alluded to this, and the more recent contributions of Mackenzie certainly underline the importance of a pro-imperial popular culture. Yet much work remains to be done on the relationship between finance, industry and the Victorian mass media.

The Burma episode of 1885 reveals another important weapon in the armoury of gentlemanly capitalist influence which has received insufficient attention. One of the key factors which prompted the British decision to invade was the revelation that the Burmese king was on the brink of signing a major treaty with the French which would have delivered to them the vast forest and mining wealth of the country, to the exclusion of British interests. This intelligence came to the British government in 1885, not through their official diplomatic channels (the British Resident in Mandalay had been withdrawn several years earlier), but through the commercial representative of the Bombay Burmah Trading Corporation, the local subsidiary of Wallace Brothers. This was an example of the kind of international informal network of intelligence which gentlemanly capitalists could place at the disposal of British politicians at times of imperial crisis. It constituted a potent method of shaping government policy and actions. Bowen makes the point that the growth of the

British empire in the eighteenth century had created a transcontinental gentlemanly capitalist elite, as British merchants settled at the imperial frontier, taking with them the gentlemanly values of home but maintaining close commercial and personal connexions with fellow gentlemanly capitalists in London.[46] From this emerged a global network which was to prove an invaluable source of intelligence for the British state as well as the financiers of London. Such control of intelligence was a powerful tool for gentlemanly capitalists to secure desirable policies from the British state. There is a resonance here with Bayly's study of intelligence networks and British rule in India, and with Darwin's stress upon links between interests in the metropole and in those at the imperial 'bridgehead' on the periphery.[47] Both of these works emphasise the importance of control over the flow of information to imperial policy makers, and how this could be crucial for steering government decisions in desirable directions, even stimulating military intervention or annexation. The point is that the international network of gentlemanly capitalists was a powerful factor in helping officialdom both in Britain and at the periphery to decide on policy. Gentlemanly capitalist power rested on more than cosy intimacy with the political elite in London. It also sprang from control of knowledge and intelligence of the wider world. The most powerful financiers enjoyed awesome leverage through this facility. Niall Ferguson demonstrates how the kinship, intelligence and business networks of Rothschilds across Europe vested that family with huge political influence, showing how gentlemanly capitalists could shape policies towards nations and territories without as well as within the empire.[48]

The debate therefore still continues about gentlemanly capitalism, and in spite of the doubts of some critics, it does seem that there is considerable scope for further exploration of the concept. The emphasis upon the role of metropolitan financial capitalism and capital exports in explaining not only the phenomenon of imperial expansion, but also the creation of the modern global economic system, has lent the thesis strong currency in the emerging contemporary debate about the nature and roots of globalisation. It is significant that the most recent explorations of gentlemanly capitalism firmly connect it to this wider theme.[49]

Japanese historians in particular have explored how Britain's expanding imperial economy from the late Victorian period impacted upon the regional Asian economy centred on China, helping to draw it into the wider global economic system.[50] The chronological range of Cain and Hopkins' work, which traces the empire up to the late twentieth century, has undoubtedly helped propel their thesis to prominence. In addition, the sheer ambition of the work will inevitably generate further debate and contention, as regional specialists scrutinise and challenge the various geographical case studies which Cain and Hopkins offer. In spite of the trenchant scepticism of many historians towards ambitious theoretical explanations of imperialism, it is fair to say that gentlemanly capitalism is one which is likely to occupy the centre stage of debate for some time yet.

Notes

1 P. J. Cain and A. G. Hopkins, *British Imperialism: Innovation and Expansion Volume 1: 1688–1914* (London, 1993); *British Imperialism: Crisis and Deconstruction Volume 2: 1914–1990* (London, 1993).

2 R. E. Dummett, *Gentlemanly Capitalism and British Imperialism: The New Debate on Empire* (London, 1999); Shigeru Akita (ed.), *Gentlemanly Capitalism, Imperialism and Global History* (Basingstoke, 2002); P. J. Cain and A. G. Hopkins, *British Imperialism 1688–2000* (London, 2001).

3 W. Hutton, *The State We're In* (London, 1995).

4 P. J. Cain and A. G. Hopkins, 'The political economy of British expansion overseas 1750 to 1914' *Economic History Review* 33:4 (1980), 463–90.

5 A. G. Hopkins, *An Economic History of West Africa* (London, 1973).

6 M. Wiener, *English Culture and the Decline of the Industrial Spirit 1850–1980* (New York, 1981).

7 W. D. Rubinstein, *Capitalism, Culture and Decline in Britain 1750–1990* (London, 1993).

8 W. D. Rubinstein, *Men of Property: The Very Wealthy in Great Britain Since the Industrial Revolution* (London, 1981).

9 N. F. R. Crafts, *British Economic Growth During the Industrial Revolution* (Oxford, 1985); W. W. Rostow, *The Stages of Economic Growth: A non-Communist Manifesto* (Cambridge, 1960).

10 C. Lee, *The British Economy Since 1700: A Macroeconomic Perspective* (Cambridge, 1986); P. K. O'Brien and C. Keyder, *Economic Growth in Britain and France 1780–1914. Two Paths to the Twentieth Century* (London, 1978); Cain and Hopkins, *British Imperialism*, p. 36.

11 A. Webster, *Gentlemen Capitalists: British Imperialism in South East Asia 1770–1890* (London, 1998).

12 Cain and Hopkins, *British Imperialism*, p. 68.

13 *Ibid.*, p. 73.
14 *Ibid.*, pp. 92–3.
15 *Ibid.*, p. 95.
16 *Ibid.*, pp. 84–5.
17 *Ibid.*, pp. 161–5.
18 *Ibid.*, pp. 122–3.
19 *Ibid.*, pp. 137–41.
20 *Ibid.*, p. 55.
21 *Ibid.*, pp. 184–202.
22 *Ibid.*, pp. 312–17.
23 For Latin America see *ibid.*, pp. 243–71; for China see pp. 360–80.
24 D. Kennedy, 'Imperial history and post colonial theory' *Journal of Imperial and Commonwealth History* 24:3 (1996), 345–63; 345.
25 D. K. Fieldhouse, 'Gentleman capitalists and the British empire' *Journal of Imperial and Commonwealth History* 22:3 (1994), 531–41; 541.
26 Cain and Hopkins, *British Imperialism*, pp. 361–2.
27 *Ibid.*, pp. 324–6.
28 See I. Phimister, 'Empire, imperialism and the partition of Africa', in S. Akita, *Gentlemanly Capitalism, Imperialism and Global History* (Basingstoke, 2002), pp. 65–82, and the response by Cain and Hopkins in the same volume, pp. 207–55, pp. 217–18.
29 Cain and Hopkins, *British Imperialism*, p. 53.
30 M. Daunton, 'Gentlemanly capitalism and British industry 1820–1914', *Past and Present* 122 (February 1989), 119–58.
31 *Ibid.*, 128–30.
32 *Ibid.*, 133.
33 *Ibid.*, 139; see also S. D. Chapman, 'British marketing enterprise: the changing role of merchants, manufacturers and financiers 1700–1860', *Business History Review* 53 (1979), 217–31.
34 W. D. Rubinstein, 'Debate: gentlemanly capitalism and British industry 1820–1914', *Past and Present* 132 (August 1991), 150–70; 169. See also Daunton's response, 170–87.
35 H. Bowen, 'Sinews of trade and empire: the supply of commodity exports to the East India Company during the late eighteenth century', *Economic History Review* 55:3 (2002), 466–86.
36 A. Webster, 'India and the colonial bank movement: the City, provinces, periphery and the abortive Indian bank schemes of 1836 to 1844' (forthcoming).
37 A. Webster, 'An early global business in a colonial context: the strategies, management and failure of John Palmer and Co. of Calcutta c. 1800 to 1830', *Enterprise and Society: The International Journal of Business History* 6:1 (March 2005), 98–133.
38 A. Webster, 'Business and empire: a reassessment of the British conquest of Burma in 1885', *Historical Journal* 43:4 (2000), 1003–25.
39 Webster, 'India and the colonial bank movement'.
40 M. Daunton, 'Gentlemanly capitalism', 146–51; D. Cannadine, 'The empire strikes back', *Past and Present* 147 (May 1995), 180–94; 190–1.
41 A. C. Howe, 'Free trade and the City of London c. 1820–1870' *History* 77:251 (October 1992), 391–410.

42 *Ibid.*, 405–7.
43 Darwin, 'Imperialism and the Victorians', 624.
44 E. H. H. Green, 'Gentlemanly capitalism and British economic policy, 1880–1914: the debate over bimetallism and protectionism', in R. E. Dummett (ed.), *Gentlemanly Capitalism and British Imperialism* (London, 1999), pp. 44–67, p. 66.
45 Webster, 'Business and empire', 1023.
46 H. Bowen, 'Gentlemanly capitalism and the making of a global British empire: some connections and contexts, 1688–1815', in Akita (ed.), *Gentlemanly Capitalism, Imperialism and Global History*, pp. 19–42.
47 C. A. Bayly, *Empire and Information: Intelligence Gathering and Social Communication in India 1780–1870* (Cambridge, 1996); Darwin, 'Imperialism and the Victorians', 641.
48 N. Ferguson, *The World's Banker: The History of the House of Rothschild* (London, 1998), pp. 5–6.
49 Akita (ed.), *Gentlemanly Capitalism, Imperialism and Global History*; Cain and Hopkins, *British Imperialism*, pp. 661–81; A. G. Hopkins, 'Back to the future: from national history to imperial history', *Past and Present* 164 (August 1999), 198–243.
50 Akita, introduction to *Gentlemanly Capitalism, Imperialism and Global History* pp. 5–6.

8

The future of Britain's imperial history?

The evolution of historical debate over the last century about the rise of the British empire has seen a radical transformation of the subject into one of the richest and most complex in the study of history. At the beginning of the twentieth century, perceptions of the British empire tended to be narrow and uncritical. The ideas of Froude and Seeley still dominated. Empire and British global dominance were taken to be the logical culmination of the ingenuity, energy and superiority of the Anglo-Saxon race and its culture. Imperial history was about how the rulers conquered, governed and uplifted subject peoples. It was in essence the history of the 'white chaps' who ruled less significant people of different colour and religion, an approach which still frustrated future historians such as Linda Colley as late as the 1970s. The concerns and culture of the conquered were at best of only passing interest to most late Victorian imperial historians. It was generally assumed that the British were purveyors of a higher stage of civilisation, which benefited all of those fortunate enough to be brought under the Union flag.

The British empire as a subject of historical enquiry at the end of the twentieth century would have been almost unrecognisable to most late Victorian scholars. Most striking was the sea change in the tone of writing on empire. No longer was it seen as an expression of British success and moral superiority. Instead, it had become synonymous with aggression, exploitation, racism and the worst excesses of human behaviour. A vast literature on the political, economic, social and cultural consequences of empire, much of it critical in tone, had been published. It was rich in both regional and academic specialisation. Large numbers of books and journal articles existed both on individual colonies and on different aspects of their history. Some of these would have been unintelligible to a late Victorian historian. Even the definition of imperialism would have been difficult to comprehend, encompassing as it did notions of 'informal empire'. One can only imagine his (for our historian would almost certainly have been male) puzzlement and consternation at such concepts as feminism, popular culture, orientalism and ornamentalism. This survey of that process of academic evolution is inevitably selective and imperfect, such is the sheer volume of work published about the rise of the British empire. It is useful, however, to consider some of the principal factors which have shaped the literature on the subject.

History, of course, can never be written from a perspective of complete objectivity. The work of the historian is inevitably influenced by the contemporary concerns of the world which he or she inhabits. New areas of historical interest emerge, and older ones are jettisoned, in perpetually shifting attempts to make sense of the modern world by the re-examination of its roots in the old. This is the reason why the subject is dynamic, why each new generation revisits the past afresh. The past is both 're-inventible' and disposable, as new versions of history are created in an effort to explain the current state of affairs. The ways in which British imperial histories have been constructed by writers and historians in the twentieth century clearly demonstrates these trends. Witness for example Hobson's and Lenin's explanations of British imperialism, which were driven by a desire to explain respectively, the origins of Edwardian Britain's economic crisis, and the First World War. Similarly, Gallagher and Robinson's interpretation of imperialism, especially their focus on 'informal empire', was partly guided by observation of the exercise of American global power after 1945. Underpinning the concept of 'gentlemanly capitalism' offered by Cain and Hopkins, is an intellectual attempt to account for the decline of Britain as an industrial power, especially from the 1960s–1970s. Interest in imperialism from the perspectives of feminism and popular culture, reflected the democratisation, liberalisation and growing affluence of the western capitalist societies in which many historians lived. The emergence of national independence movements in the colonies during the twentieth century challenged the racist assumptions of the old imperial order, and large-scale immigration into Britain from South Asia and the Caribbean after 1950, led to the challenge of racist ideas in Britain itself. This contributed hugely to the shift in perceptions of British imperialism from great civilising mission to racist oppressor.

Academic and intellectual trends were also instrumental in refashioning perceptions of the British empire. The international proliferation of universities and academic historians, especially after 1945, unleashed an unprecedented expansion of research, which opened new archives and historical sources. Nationalist historians in the former colonies challenged residual notions of the benign character of British colonial rule. New intellectual approaches revolutionised the tools of historical analysis. Marxist ideas on empire, pioneered by Lenin were taken up by the academic community. After the Second World War a new British Marxist tradition of 'history from below' which looked at the history of the subordinate classes of society, pioneered by such historians as E. P. Thompson, began to be applied to the peoples of the empire. In the 1960s 'New Left' historians and sociologists were arguing that much of the less developed world's poverty and inequality had been caused by the effects of centuries of European imperial exploitation. Sociological concepts, feminist ideas, postmodernist notions borrowed from philosophy, as well as new techniques of statistical economic analysis, all provided in their turn, new ways of evaluating the causes and consequences of the rise of the British empire.

Furthermore, although it is almost fifty years after the effective demise of the British empire, there is little sign that awareness of and concern about its legacy is diminishing. Britain's multi-ethnic society, high profile involvement in military leadership and adventures, and the occasional eruption of controversy or trouble surrounding the rump of possessions still in British hands (the Falklands and Gibraltar), have all ensured that several post-imperial generations have remained in touch with Britain's former global role. As seen, in the academic world, interest in Britain's imperialist experience seems to have gone from strength to strength, and shows no sign of abating. Just as Gallagher and

Robinson's work gave rise to a new school of research and debate in the 1950s, both Said's post-colonial theory and the gentlemanly capitalism thesis of Cain and Hopkins have breathed new life into the study of the British empire. What seem to be the likely avenues of future enquiry? What clues do we have about coming trends in the study of the subject?

International events since the end of the Cold War have certainly prompted reassessments of the British empire. Western triumphalism at the demise of communism, and predictions of an 'end of history' in the establishment of a permanent world order of liberal democratic capitalism swiftly proved to be premature and over-optimistic.[1] Hopes that a reinforced western global hegemony would usher in a new era of international peace, prosperity and democracy were quickly dashed in the 1990s by serious episodes of violence, warfare, genocide, terrorism and social collapse in sub-Saharan Africa, Yugoslavia, Chechnya, Palestine and Afghanistan. 'Rogue' states such as Iraq, the Taliban dominated regime in Afghanistan and the residual Stalinist regime in North Korea all obdurately defied the new world order. The destruction of the World Trade Centre in New York on 11 September 2001 dispelled any remaining illusions that global harmony was at hand. American- and British-led interventions in Kuwait, Bosnia, Kosovo and Sierra Leone had already suggested that a new world order would have to be imposed rather than emerge. The events of 9/11 precipitated further interventions in Afghanistan and Iraq, and gave rise to the view in some quarters that a new era of American imperialism was beginning. Predictably, the response of the left and liberal opinion has been extremely critical of the USA, but some voices have spoken in favour of a new age of empire, calling for the USA to impose order on those poor and less developed parts of the world (principally in the middle east and sub-Saharan Africa) where anarchy threatens prospects for stability and economic development. In itself this is quite a startling development. Ever since the end of the Second World War, the dominant intellectual trends have been sharply critical of imperialism. Even when the USA asserted its power in Vietnam in the 1960s, and the USSR invaded Afghanistan in 1980, political and intellectual supporters denied both imperialist motives and the imperial character of these actions. Since 9/11, however, some western commentators have openly supported a new American imperialism. Among these, the historian Professor Niall Ferguson (b. 1964) has emerged as perhaps the most influential exponent.

Already a celebrated Oxford financial historian before moving to take up prestigious positions at first New York and then Harvard universities, Ferguson has established a powerful presence in the mass media in Britain and the USA as a commentator on current affairs, and his views have even been sought by the White House.[2] Ferguson, whose views are firmly on the political right, built his reputation with a series of books on financial history, including a masterly study of the Rothschild family. In 2002–3 he turned his attention to the history of the British empire, producing both a best selling book and a major British TV series on the subject.[3] This was rapidly followed by a second book on the American empire, which was also turned into a British TV series.[4] Both books emphasise the similarities between the British and American versions of imperialism; a central argument of Ferguson's is that modern US administrations have much to learn from the principles, methods and personnel used to run the former British empire. As with so many historians of empire, Ferguson's interest in the subject stemmed in part from personal experience. His grandfather, uncle and father had all worked in various colonies, while Ferguson cites vivid childhood memories of post-colonial Kenya.[5] Though a Scot born in empire's twilight, for Ferguson it stood in 'bright sunlight'.[6] Such was the young Ferguson's affection for empire that he enraged a student audience in an Oxford Union debate in 1982 by opposing the motion 'This House Regrets Colonisation'.[7] Ferguson's enthusiasm for relating history to contemporary issues infuses nearly all of his work. For example, *The Cash Nexus* is all about explaining the historical origins of the modern world financial system, and how these have shaped political developments.[8] Ferguson is no determinist. He believes that historical events and developments can follow many different trajectories, and that human agency is usually the most important factor dictating outcomes. Perhaps the most vivid expression of this has been his fascination with 'virtual history', projections of imagined alternative historical scenarios which might have become reality had this or that person, organisation or nation behaved differently.[9] It is an approach which exemplifies Ferguson's belief that what actually happened in the past was not inevitable and that history has real lessons to teach those who shape and govern the contemporary world.

In sharp contrast to nearly half a century of predominantly critical assessments of the British empire, Ferguson offers not only a spirited defence of British imperialism, but also support for the USA to lead a new age of empire. In *Empire* Ferguson draws upon the rich historical literature on empire to chart the growth, governance and ideological development of British imperialism. But the significance of the book lies in its concluding chapters, which offer a sturdy defence of the British imperial record, on a number of counts. Firstly, Ferguson contends that the British empire of the nineteenth and early twentieth centuries was pivotal in the creation of an international system of free trade which facilitated the huge growth of the world economy during the period. The empire also promoted the free international movement of capital and labour which were also crucial in the development of the modern international capitalist system.[10] Secondly, Ferguson dismisses the notion, supported by many of the 'New Left', that the British empire 'underdeveloped' its colonies in Africa and Asia. He argues that under British rule, their potential for growth and development was realised to a high degree, and where results were disappointing this was frequently due to limitations of climate, terrain or resource availability – problems which were only marginally susceptible to alleviation by the actions of the colonial state. Ferguson argues that the legal and administrative principles imposed by the British were particularly beneficial in stimulating growth, because they provided order and protected property in a relatively disinterested and impartial way. This ensured a secure environment in which business could be conducted and vital foreign investment attracted to the colony. In contrast, the period of decolonisation after the Second World War saw the political fragmentation of many former colonies, with civil wars, the destruction of legal and political order, and the emergence of corrupt or bankrupt regimes, too poor or inadequately endowed with resources to achieve economic viability or decent living standards for their populations. Far from causing the miseries of Africa and Asia after decolonisation, the British empire had provided the best environment for the progress of these colonies, and independence had in many instances swept away the advantages which imperial rule had bestowed. Thirdly, Ferguson contends that in the twentieth century, the British empire offered an infinitely preferable system to the rival imperialisms of Nazi Germany or Imperial Japan. Ferguson cites Hitler's comment that Indians would face a far bleaker future under Nazi imperial rule than under the British.[11] Furthermore, the British empire was instrumental in the defeat of these more aggressive and ruthless imperial powers – ultimately at the price of its own demise. Ferguson acknowledges that British rule certainly displayed less benevolent aspects – slavery and racism in particular. But for him, the balance weighs heavily towards a favourable assessment of the effects of the British empire on the subject peoples of the colonies, and the world in general. In this conclusion, Ferguson is at odds with the view of B. R. Tomlinson, whose recent contribution to the *Oxford History of the British Empire*, sees mainly the colonies of European settlement as the principal beneficiaries of empire in economic terms.[12] In contrast, Tomlinson concludes that 'British rule did not leave a substantial legacy of wealth, health, or happiness to the majority of the subjects of the Commonwealth'.[13]

Ferguson is also upbeat about the value of the empire for Britain itself. For him, the British empire was an experiment in 'Anglobalisation', in which a new world order of free trade and free capital movement proved hugely advantageous to British merchants, industrialists and investors.[14] This runs against the grain of most previous alternative assessments of the impact of the empire on the British economy. Certainly, the jaundiced assessment of the effects of British imperialism and the export of capital associated with it offered by Hobson, has largely been rejected. In the 1980s, two economic historians at the California Institute of Technology, Lance Davis and Robert Huttenback undertook an exhaustive econometric analysis of the economic gains and costs of the British empire.[15] While this comprehensively dismissed the notion that export of capital to the empire starved British industry of investment, it concluded that imperial possessions provided few material benefits for the British economy. Davis and Huttenback contend, moreover, that the costs of empire fell disproportionately as high levels of tax on the British middle class, while her aristocracy and the financial elite in the City of London benefited substantially from the secure returns on overseas investment. Starkly they concluded that empire was little more than 'a mechanism for transferring income from the middle to the upper classes'.[16] At almost the same time, Patrick O'Brien (b. 1932), then Reader in Economic History at the University of Oxford and now Centennial Professor of Economic History at the London School of Economics, reached very similar conclusions in respect of the period 1840 to 1914.[17] Empire not only redirected income from poor to rich and stifled enterprise with heavy taxation, it also insulated industry from the necessary pressures of foreign competition by providing safe imperial markets for British exports. Moreover, obsession with defending the empire hampered the British ability to prepare effectively for a European war, thereby hampering efforts to deter German militarism. On all of these counts, O'Brien concludes that costs substantially outweighed benefits. Even Fieldhouse's more favourable re-evaluation of empire's impact on the British economy for the *Oxford History of the British Empire* in 1999, concedes that these were modest, ambiguous and in no way essential for British economic success before 1914.[18] In the context of these earlier, critical accounts of the value of empire for the British themselves, Ferguson's conclusions are, as in other respects, controversial.

Even more provocative is Ferguson's call for a new American imperium, based on many of the principles of imperial governance pioneered by the British.[19] In the comparison between the American and British empires, of course, Ferguson is following a well trodden path. Gallagher and Robinson in the 1950s were among the earliest to see close parallels between the methods through which the two countries conducted their imperial affairs. It is a trend which has been encouraged by the trans-Atlantic exchange of academics – see for example the acknowledged influence of the experience of the USA on the work of Colley and Cannadine. Ferguson applies his comparative analysis to very current and controversial issues. Ferguson urges the US to 'prepare for the long haul' in their occupation of Iraq, and refers to the British experience in Egypt after 1882 as an example of what may be required. Such an outspoken advocacy of the supposed virtues of imperialism as a solution to global problems of economic development represents a sharp break with the condemnatory tone of most writing on imperialism since the Second World War. Responses to Ferguson's ideas have therefore been predictably critical. Andrew Porter, for example, derides Ferguson's tendency to give 'rough justice to complexity', and criticises Ferguson's 'whiggish' inclination to put a bright gloss on the development of the empire. For Porter, Ferguson's approach is neither new nor adequate, a view shared by numerous critics of Ferguson's work.[20] But while Ferguson remains a relatively isolated voice, it will be interesting to see if other historians and intellectuals follow his lead. The demise of communism and the general retreat of Leftist ideology may well allow space for new 'pro-imperial' histories of empire. As shown below, the current academic focus on globalisation has rekindled interest in the role of empires in helping to create an integrated world economy – and it should be remembered that globalisation has its supporters as well as its detractors. On the other hand of course, the controversy surrounding American- and British-led invasion of Iraq in 2003, and the troubled events which have followed, have prompted something of a backlash, which has expressed itself in part through reflection on earlier failed episodes of imperial intervention in the middle east, such as Suez in 1956. Together these contradictory trends in opinion about the legacy of empire seem likely to provoke a much livelier debate about the effects and moral consequences of British imperialism than when a monolithic consensus of condemnation was the norm.

The work of Cain and Hopkins also prompts speculation about forthcoming research and insights into British imperialism. The breadth of their work, and the fierce controversies which have erupted over it, promise ongoing debate for some time to come. Several aspects of it particularly seem ripe for further exploration. Firstly, the question of the relative positions of industrial and financial capital in Britain remains an important area of contention. While Rubinstein as well as Cain and Hopkins provides a convincing case for the superiority in terms of wealth of the City of London, the ability of industrialists to exert political influence in imperial affairs, and their relations with London gentlemanly capitalists, are fields which require much more archival research. The most promising sources for this are the private papers and commercial records of both financiers and industrialists, the papers of the numerous parliamentary select committees which examined trade in detail, and the minutes and records of the commercial pressure groups, associations and chambers of commerce of the various towns and cities of Britain and the empire. The latter in particular are an under-used source, yet they offer to reveal much about both the political influence of industrialists and their relations with the gentlemanly capitalists of the City, and interests on the periphery of empire. In the early 1960s, some work was done on links between British chambers of commerce and their counterparts in Calcutta, Singapore and other parts of the far east, but surprisingly little has been done since then.[21] Yet herein almost certainly lies important evidence with which to test the Cain and Hopkins thesis, especially for the period when industry made its political clout felt most acutely, in the first half of the nineteenth century.

Other fields for future study which are opening as a result of the Cain and Hopkins thesis include the nature of power as exercised by nations over others, and the emergence of a globalised economic system. On the first of these, Cain and Hopkins have refined some of their earlier arguments. In particular they have sought to identify two ways in which dominant imperial powers assert themselves. The first of these is through what they call 'structural power', or the international rules which govern commerce, diplomacy and all aspects of relations between nations. Cain and Hopkins have in mind here the regime of free trade, international law and adoption of 'responsible' principles of governance and economic management (such as balanced budgets and low taxation) by financially dependent countries, which was imposed by the British on much of the international community in the nineteenth century.[22] By controlling the framework which governed the conduct of international relations, the British were able to ensure that weaker nations accommodated the needs of British commerce and wider interests. In addition, there was also 'relational power', the particular negotiated relations between Britain and these subordinate powers, the treaties, alliances or other agreements which determined British relations with the specific country concerned. Cain and Hopkins seem to be trying here to provide a keener definition of the concept of informal rule, one which seeks to account for how subordinate nations could exercise a measure of independence from Britain's imperial dominance in some areas, whilst complying in other more important ones, such as commercial or strategic impera- tives. They argue that British relations with the white dominions, for example, can be best understood in light of this dual concept of power. The value of this contribution, of course, is not restricted to study of the British empire. Insights into the complexities of the exercise of informal influence might be equally applicable, for example, to the rise and maintenance of American hegemony since the Second World War. Certainly it is easy to see how post-war international institutions such as the World Bank, the International Monetary Fund and the General Agreement on Tariffs and Trade might be viewed as components of a new, American dominated framework of structural power. In this respect, the contribution of Cain and Hopkins to the study of empire will almost certainly extend beyond British imperialism.

In fact their work has already stepped beyond the confines of British imperial history. In the concluding chapter of the second edition of their book, published in 2001, Cain and Hopkins discuss the relationship between imperialism and the rise of a globalised economy and culture by the end of the twentieth century.[23] For them empires in general were agents of the creation of not only a world economic system, but also other major cultural phenomena, such as the emergence of the nation state, and the mutual shaping of cultures as a result of prolonged contact with the 'other'. Cain and Hopkins are not alone in this stress upon imperialism as the forger of global systems of human interaction. Linda Colley emphasised the importance of empires in developing 'connexity', the complex linkages between different societies, cultures and peoples which were themselves a major factor in shaping the histories of superficially separate nation- states.[24] Colley argues that the study of all imperial histories, not just the modern or British varieties, offers a way out of the strait- jacket of compartmentalised national or regional histories. Contemplation of the multi-national and multi-cultural dimensions of imperial history brings into sharper focus the often subtle but vital global shifts and trends which shaped the development of countries and continents, but which frequently fall below the restricted horizons of the narrow national or even regional historian. Like Colley, though their work focuses mainly upon the British empire, Cain and Hopkins see other imperialisms as playing a crucial role in the emergence of the modern globalised economy and culture. For Cain and Hopkins do not regard the origins of globalisation as recent. Drawing on the work of other historians in the field, they argue that four distinct phases can be identified in the creation of the modern global system, phases which may be dated back centuries.

The first of these was a period of 'archaic globalised networks', which can be located in the emergence of some of the early empires associated with all-encompassing religious movements with expansionist ambitions; namely Christianity, Islam, Hinduism and Buddhism.[25] While these early attempts to create a world system made some headway through cultural and demographic diasporas as well as trade, the technological limits of the time, which made distance and communication a weak point in these aspiring attempts at globalisation, ensured that their duration and impact was always constrained. The Americas and Australasia, for example, remained completely outside their orbit. After 1600, a second phase of globalising trends has been identified, the defining features of which were the emergence of more robust state systems of revenue/resource collection and administration than existed previously, together with more sophisticated economic development in the areas of finance and pre-industrial manufacturing. These innovations provided both the means and the impetus for a new era of globalising imperialist activity, referred to as 'proto-globalisation'. The European imperial expansions of Spain, Portugal, Holland, France and of course Britain in the period 1600 to 1800 fall under this category, as does the spread of the Ottoman empire into Northern Africa and south eastern Europe, and the growth of Chinese imperial power in the far east. Again, however, limitations of technology, particular in warfare, ensured that its impact, though more extensive and intrusive than its archaic predecessor, was constrained. After 1800, however, the third phase of globalising development, 'modern globalisation' was much more invasive. Two attributes made this possible: the rise of the nation-state and industrialisation. The first heightened the aggressiveness of European imperial expansion through its emphasis upon notions of national or racial superiority, while the second increased its effectiveness through greater economic penetration in the search for raw materials and markets, and through better communications and military superiority for the imperialist powers. In this phase, European imperialism reigned supreme as the vehicle for globalisation, though resistance from local societies and European rivalries checked the degree to which a truly global market and culture could emerge. The most recent phase of globalisation occurred after the demise of most of the European empires, and is consequently referred to as 'post-colonial' globalisation. This is in many senses paradoxical, because while decolonisation meant that the structures of formal imperial control were removed from the former colonies, to be replaced by new forms of national government, the welding together of the global economy, and the consolidation of an increasingly globalised international culture gathered pace. New technologies of communication, the rise of globally organised trans-national corporations and the emergence of global financial and economic institutions (the IMF, the World Bank etc) resulted in greater global integration than ever before. The West's victory in the Cold War accelerated this process, to the extent that by the early twenty-first century, debate had moved onto whether or not the nation-state was now powerless in the face of the new global political and economic order.

Cain and Hopkins' stress upon the role of gentlemanly capitalism and financial imperialism offers to help explain the emergence of a globalised international order, and it seems certain that a future theme in the study of imperialism generally will focus upon the relationship between empire and globalising trends. Two areas in particular seem to beckon. First, a concern related to the rise of a modern globalised economy is its impact upon the increasingly fragile ecology of the planet. Deforestation and global warming have largely replaced nuclear annihilation as the spectres of future catastrophes. Historians have only recently begun to turn their attention to the earlier impact of imperialism and economic expansion on global ecology. Crucial in this was

Crosby's *Ecological Imperialism: The Biological Expansion of Europe 900–1900* which examined how European expansion fundamentally altered the world's flora and fauna.[26] Grove, Gadgil and Guha, Mackenzie, Griffiths and Robin, and Mann have all mapped out various aspects of this theme, but the scope for further research is enormous, and likely to expand hugely in future years.[27] The second area concerns the potentially vast field of comparative imperial history. Much writing on European empires tends to focus upon individual national imperialisms, with relatively few comparative studies which try to identify common trends or differences. As interest in empire becomes increasingly linked to the question of globalisation, we can expect to see much more work in this vital yet under-developed branch of the scholarship of imperialism.

As seen, the field of culture and imperialism has developed substantially since Said's groundbreaking work in the 1970s. John Mackenzie and the Manchester University Press series *Studies in Imperialism* have played a crucial role in leading what has been a revolution in imperial history since the 1980s, and doubtless will continue to forge ahead with new ideas and initiatives in years to come. In particular, Colley, Cannadine and others have amply demonstrated that British interactions with the conquered peoples of the empire were based on much more than racism or notions of cultural superiority, and that these varied across British social groups and over time. However, there is much more work to be done on the role of women and social class in all empires, and surprisingly race and British imperialism has yet to generate the overarching monograph the subject demands. Several recent works in particular offer signposts for future directions of enquiry. Bayly's work on the way in which imperial channels of intelligence and communication shaped imperial policy in India needs to be repeated for other colonial contexts, a project which incidentally offers to throw much light upon the debates about gentlemanly capitalism and its influence.[28] Hall's *Civilising Subjects* also provides an excellent case study which explores the interaction between groups and individuals in the metropole and the periphery over a substantial period of time, demonstrating how these shaped and changed views over time. Hall provides a dynamic vision of imperial attitudes, culture and policies, which captures their fluidity and the sophistication of the processes of change which these underwent. It is an approach which offers much by its application to other periods and other colonies, and the benefits for understanding wider questions of imperial policy formation, the developing relations between interest groups at the heart and on the edge of empire, as well as such phenomena as globalisation, are almost incalculable.

A brief scan through the five volumes of the recently published *The Oxford History of the British Empire* provides an insight into the current state of the study of the British empire. What is striking is not merely the geographical breadth and depth of scholarship in discussing the effects of empire on so many parts of the world, but also the range of different approaches – economic, social, cultural and environmental. Together these have provided the subject with a vibrancy perhaps lacking when Linda Colley ruefully reflected on the dominance of the 'white chaps' in teaching and subject matter in the early 1970s. The continuing work of the Manchester University series *Studies in Imperialism* promises to further enrich the subject. Coupled with this, the transparent relevance of the study of empire to contemporary themes such as American power, globalisation and the cultural contacts and conflicts it generates, ensures that it is certainly one of the most dynamic fields of historical research and writing. It is therefore unsurprising that the study of the rise of the British empire shows no sign of faltering in intensity. Growing concerns in the early twenty-first century with the position of the nation state in an increasingly interdependent world economy, seemingly intractable global problems of inequality and poverty and continuing expressions of quasi-imperial power by states such as the USA, all promise to keep the study of imperialism high on the academic agenda. As long as this remains the case, the British empire, with its striking geographical, ideological and chronological span, will attract an international field of scholarship. The British empire will continue to rise, at least in the mountain of books and articles which will still grow, generations after the sun has finally set upon the last British colony.

Notes

1 See, for example, F. Fukuyama, *The End of History and the Last Man* (London, 1992).
2 'US loves a home truths kinda guy', *The Times Higher Education Supplement*, 21 May 2004.
3 N. Ferguson, *Empire: How Britain Made the Modern World* (London, 2003).
4 N. Ferguson, *Colossus: The Rise and Fall of the American Empire* (London, 2004).
5 Ferguson, *Empire*, pp. xiv–xv.
6 *Ibid.*, p. xvi.
7 *Ibid.*, p. xvii.
8 N. Ferguson, *The Cash Nexus: Money and Power in the Modern World 1700–2000* (London, 2001).
9 N. Ferguson (ed.), *Virtual History* (London, 1998).
10 Ferguson, *Empire* pp. 367–8.
11 *Ibid.*, p. 335.
12 B. R. Tomlinson, 'Imperialism and after: the economy of the empire on the periphery' in J. M. Brown and W. R. Louis, *The Oxford History of the British Empire: Volume 4: The Twentieth Century* (Oxford, 1999), pp. 357–78.
13 *Ibid.*, p. 375.
14 Ferguson, *Empire*, p. xxiv and p. 325.
15 L. E. Davis and R. Huttenback, *Mammon and the Pursuit of Empire: The Political Economy of British Imperialism* (Cambridge, 1987).
16 *Ibid.*, p. 279.
17 P. K. O'Brien, 'The costs and benefits of British imperialism 1846–1914', *Past and Present* 120 (1988), 163–200.
18 D. K. Fieldhouse, 'The metropolitan economics of empire', in J. M. Brown and W. R. Louis, *The Oxford History of the British Empire: Volume 4*, pp. 88–113; p. 111.
19 Ferguson, *Colossus*, ch. 6.
20 Online review of *Empire* by Professor Andrew Porter for the Institute of Historical Research, at www.history.ac.uk/reviews/paper/porterA.html.
21 I. Nish, 'British mercantile co-operation in the Indo-Chine trade from the end of the East India Company's trading monopoly', *Journal of Southeast Asian History* 3:2 (1962), 74–91.
22 Cain and Hopkins, 'Afterword', in Dummett (ed.), *Gentlemanly Capitalism and Imperialism*, pp. 204–5.
23 Cain and Hopkins, *British Imperialism*, pp. 662–81.
24 L.Colley, 'What is imperial history now?' in D. Cannadine (ed.), *What is History Now?* (London, 2002), pp. 132–47; p. 134 and pp. 138–41.
25 See A. G. Hopkins, 'Introduction: globalization – an agenda for historians', in A. G. Hopkins (ed.), *Globalization in World History* (London, 2002), pp. 1–10; pp. 4–5.
26 A. W. Crosby, *Ecological Imperialism: The Biological Expansion of Europe 900–1900* (Cambridge, 1986).
27 R. Grove, *Green Imperialism: Colonial Expansion, Tropical Island Edens and the Origins of Environmentalism, 1600–1860* (Cambridge, 1995); M. Gadgil and R. Guha, *The Fissured Land: An Ecological History of India* (Delhi,

1992); J. M. Mackenzie, *The Empire of Nature: Hunting, Conservation and British Imperialism* (Manchester, 1988); T. Griffiths and L. Robin, *Ecology and Empire: Environmental History of Settler Societies* (Edinburgh, 1997); M. Mann, *British Rule on Indian Soil* (New Delhi, 1999).
28 C. A. Bayly, *Empire and Information* (Cambridge, 1996).

FURTHER READING

Most of the historiographical works listed here have been mentioned in the footnotes. They have been grouped together by topic for convenience:

General

Colley, L., 'What is imperial history now?', in D. Cannadine (ed.), *What is History Now?* (London, 2002), pp. 132–47.
Hodgart, A., *The Economics of European Imperialism* (London, 1977).
Louis, W. R. (ed.), *The Gallagher and Robinson Controversy* (New York, 1976).
Mommsen, W. J., *Theories of Imperialism* (London, 1980).
Samuel, R., 'Empire stories, the imperial and the domestic', in R. Samuel, *Island Stories. Unravelling Britain. Theatres of Memory Vol 2.* (London, 1998), pp. 74–97.
Simmons, J., *Parish and Empire: Studies and Sketches* (London, 1952).
Winks, R. W. (ed.), *The Oxford History of the British Empire Volume V: Historiography* (Oxford, 1999).

Pre-twentieth-century ideas on empire

Armitage, D., *The Ideological Origins of the British Empire* (Cambridge, 2000).
Cain, P. J. (ed.), *Empire and Imperialism: The Debate of the 1870s* (South Bend, IN, 1999).
Knorr, K. E., *British Colonial Theories 1570–1850* (Toronto, 1944).
Winch, D., *Classical Political Economy and Colonies* (London, 1965).

The Hobson–Lenin Debate

Barone, C. A., *Marxist Thought on Imperialism: Survey and Critique* (Basingstoke, 1985).
Barratt Brown, M., *The Economics of Imperialism* (Harmondsworth, 1974), pp. 48–72.
Cain, P., *Hobson and Imperialism: Radicalism, New Liberalism and Finance 1887–1938* (Oxford, 2002).
Cain, P., 'J. A. Hobson, financial capitalism and imperialism in late Victorian and Edwardian England', in *Journal of Imperial and Commonwealth History* 13:3 (1985), 1–27.
Eckstein, A. M., 'Is there a "Hobson-Lenin thesis" on late nineteenth-century colonial expansion?', *Economic History Review* 44 (1991), 297–318.
Hodgart, A., *The Economics of European Imperialism*, pp. 13–53.
McLellan, D., *Karl Marx: His Life and Thought* (London, 1983).
Mommsen, W. J., *Theories of Imperialism*, pp. 29–57.

Gallagher and Robinson and informal empire

Darwin, J., 'Imperialism and the Victorians: the dynamics of territorial expansion', *English Historical Review* (June 1997), 614–42.

Louis, W. R., 'Introduction', in R. W. Winks (ed.), *The Oxford History of the British Empire Volume V: Historiography* (Oxford, 1999).

Platt, D. C. M., 'The imperialism of free trade: some reservations', *Economic History Review* 21 (1968), 298–306.

Platt, D. C. M., 'Further objections to an imperialism of free trade', *Economic History Review* 26 (1973), 153–160.

Low, A., 'W. K. Hancock' (obituary), *Proceedings of the British Academy* 82, 399–414.

MacDonagh, O., 'The anti-imperialism of free trade', *Economic History Review* 14 (1962), 489–501.

Mommsen, W. J., *Theories of Imperialism*, pp. 86–93.

Shepperson, G., 'Ronald Robinson: scholar and good companion', *Journal of Imperial and Commonwealth History* 16:3 (1988), 1–8.

Culture and imperialism: post-colonial theory

Chakravorty Spivak, G., 'Subaltern studies, deconstructing historiography', in R. Guha (ed.), *Subaltern Studies IV* (Delhi, 1985).

Guha, R., 'On aspects of the historiography of colonial India', in R. Guha (ed.), *Subaltern Studies I. Writings on South Asian History and Society* (Delhi, 1982).

Kennedy, D., 'Imperial history and post-colonial theory', *Journal of Imperial and Commonwealth History* 24:3 (1996), 345–63.

Mackenzie, J. *Orientalism: History Theory and the Arts* (Manchester, 1995).

Washbrook, D. 'Orients and occidents: colonial discourse theory and the historiography of the British empire', in Winks (ed.), *The Oxford History of the British Empire Vol V*, pp. 596–611.

Culture and imperialism: race, religion and class

Etherington, N., 'Missions and empire', in Winks (ed.), *The Oxford History of the British Empire Volume V: Historiography*, pp. 303–14.

Rich, P., *Race and Empire in British Politics* (Cambridge, 1986).

Wylie, D., 'Disease, diet and gender: late twentieth-century perspectives on empire', in Winks (ed.), *The Oxford History of the British Empire: Volume V Historiography*, pp. 277–89.

Gentlemanly capitalism

Akita, S. (ed.), *Gentlemanly Capitalism, Imperialism and Global History* (Basingstoke, 2002).

Cain, P. J. and A. G. Hopkins, *British Imperialism 1688–2000* (London, 2001).

Daunton, M., 'Gentlemanly capitalism and British industry 1820–1914', *Past and Present* 122 (February 1989), 119–58.

Dummett, R. E., *Gentlemanly Capitalism and British Imperialism: The New Debate on Empire* (London, 1999).

Fieldhouse, D. K., 'Gentleman capitalists and the British empire', *Journal of Imperial and Commonwealth History* 22:3 (1994), 531–41.

INDEX

Note: 'n.' after a page reference indicates the number of a note on that page